Owls

JOHN SPARKS and TONY SOPER

Illustrated by Robert Gillmor

David & Charles

For SALLY and HILARY

British Library Cataloguing in Publication Data

Sparks, John
   Owls. – 2nd ed.
   I. Title   II. Soper, Tony
   598'.97

   ISBN 0–7153–0423–2

First published 1970
Second impression 1972
Third impression 1973
Fourth impression 1975
Fifth impression 1976
Sixth impression 1977
Seventh impression 1978
Eighth impression 1979
Ninth impression 1982
Tenth impression 1985
Second edition 1989
Reprinted 1991
First paperback edition 1995
Reprinted 1996

Printed and bound in Great Britain by
Butler & Tanner Ltd, Frome and London
for David & Charles
Brunel House   Newton Abbot   Devon

Contents

Introduction

Owls are soft-plumaged, short-tailed, big-headed birds of prey with large eyes directed forwards and surrounded by a facial disc. They are mainly nocturnal, and the one hundred and thirty-four living species (four are historically extinct) are placed in the order *Strigiformes*. Within this order there are two families: the Cosmopolitan barn (*Tyto* sp) and Afro-Asian bay owls (*Phodilus* sp) constituting the *Tytonidae*; the remaining 124 kinds are grouped in the family *Strigidae*, sub-divided into sub-families 'small-eared' *Buboninae* and 'big-eared' *Striginae*.

But in non-scientific terms, an owl is a cat with wings. It is a creature superbly adapted for hunting small rodents, watching silently till the time for the fast approach and the moment of truth. Yet, like the cat, it can be noisy on occasions, rending the night with a never-ending series of raucous courting screams and hoots. Like the cat, it is a special favourite with people.

Amongst animal toys, the owl is significantly popular. Although admittedly not in the teddy-bear class, it is nevertheless a top seller, and it is interesting to consider why this should be so. In order to be a successful toy, an animal has to be a caricature of man. It must share certain features with us such as having a vertical posture and a flat face with big eyes in the front. Go into a toyshop and you will find hardly any reptiles or amphibians—most toys come from the birds and from the mammals to which we ourselves belong. The few reptiles and amphibians will have been distorted into a shape which gives them as nearly human characteristics as possible.

Vertical posture is the most important thing, and amongst birds the two most popular toys are penguins and owls. Penguins, as little gentlemen waddling around in dinner jackets, are only too obviously humanoid, but the owl poses a much more interesting case. The toy owl is a top seller, yet when you consider the real, live owl it probably comes as near as anything to a bird version of the wolf in sheep's clothing. It is a killer, and killers are not by virtue of that fact endearing to us. But the owl hides the tools of his trade beneath soft billowing plumage; the cruel talons are hidden beneath trouser feathers, the cruel beak projects downwards from the face feathers just where the nose should be. Having successfully disguised his true personality, the owl faces the world with an upright, cuddly, human posture, with a cheek-like facial disc, great round eyes and little ear-tufts. It is no wonder that an owl-toy is a winner.

But in spite of his real-life predatory functions and his unhappy reputation as a bearer of bad news and general gloom, the owl is a fascinating bird. In this book we have tried to gather together the facts about the true bird and the legends of the mythical bird.

1 *Design for the Darkness*

Owls are pre-eminently birds of twilight and darkness, and when the dwindling light of day sends most birds flighting swiftly to their roosts the majority of owls are galvanising themselves into action in their daytime hideaways, with yawns, blinks and wing stretches. While other birds are passing away the time as gently throbbing balls of feathers, the nocturnal owl must earn its living, finding enough food to survive, and defending its territory against both space-hungry neighbours and wandering owls only too willing to stake a claim where the hunting is good. There may, too, be the business of wooing a mate, or of meeting the almost insatiable demands of fluffy owlets. All these activities may be carried out under cover of the night sky when the woods, pastures or wetlands may be, at best, only glazed by the silvery glow of the full moon. More often than not, even this aid to navigation and prey-finding will be dimmed by clouds, or the moon will be competing elsewhere with the sun.

There are, of course, owls that hunt by the light of day, and of these more will be written later. The majority of owls, however, are strictly nocturnal or crepuscular, and this fact alone has caused both poets and naturalists to marvel at their habits. Most of us would be lost if we had to live in relative darkness; when the light of the sun wanes we have to flood our homes, offices, and city streets with artificial light, and though it in no way matches the intensity or quality of sunlight, it does relieve us of total dependence upon the sun and variations of light due to weather and season. Because light to us is almost synonymous with life we assume too readily that there can be no other world but our strongly illuminated one, and that animals which live 'outside' our world are eccentric or possess strange supernormal powers. And yet the world as perceived by animals depends upon the sense organs they have and the use they make of them.

For example, bats with their sophisticated sonar apparatus and highly developed ears are able to find their way around in absolute darkness, weaving in and out of obstructions and intercepting moths; a bat lives in a world of echoes and, if able to, would describe its surroundings in terms of sounds. Those reflected from a moth tell it whether the insect was palatable and give it much other information about its texture, speed and direction of flight. There are even birds which navigate by means of echoes of their own voices, such as the oilbird of South American and several cave swiftlets; these, however, have good powers of vision, too. On the other hand, a long-nosed shrew lives in a world of smells and can, presumably, picture its surroundings by sampling the airborne chemicals with its incredibly sensitive nose. With our blunted olfactory senses, we cannot begin to understand the range and complexity of odours or what life must be like for one of these mammals. Like other primates, we live in an illuminated world of shapes and colours appreciated through our highly evolved day-vision.

There is, of course, only one world, but the relative development and dominance of eyes, ears, nose and other sense organs allow each species to glimpse their surroundings through different 'windows'. Even eyes and ears may differ in their performance between species. A bat can hear sounds beyond the sensitivity range of our own ears; the vision of an eagle is perhaps eight times more acute than our own. There is, then, a problem of imagination when we try to consider how nocturnal owls are able to live and survive during the period when we are dreaming between the bedclothes. For the

The nocturnal tarsier has large and highly developed eyes

Long-eared bat has tiny eyes and uses echo-location for hunting night flying insects

The oilbird's large eyes help it in finding food at night, but within its totally dark nesting caves it navigates by echo-location

Different groups of animals cope with the darkness in a variety of ways

Shrews have a well developed sense of smell and can "picture" the world through their long noses

success of owls as hunters depends upon their sense organs, which are adapted to work efficiently after dark and make the birds as much at home in moonlight or twilight as we are when bathed in sunshine or neon.

Apart from the abberant kiwis of New Zealand which hunt by smell—shrews of the bird world!—the lives of birds are dominated by vision. Accordingly, they have skulls which are literally built around relatively enormous eyes, and these often touch each other in the midline, at least in species with laterally facing ones. Some idea of their importance is indicated by the fact that the weight of their eyes accounts for fifteen per cent of that of their heads.

One of the most appealing features of owls is their big eyes. Their forward position on the face, together with their ability to blink with the upper (not lower, as in other birds) eyelids, gives them an uncanny, primate-like appearance. This frontal position is no accident and has great survival value for owls. Birds, like most animals, can be divided into the hunters and the hunted. The latter usually have eyes placed on the side of their narrow heads to give them all-round visibility, which greatly helps them in their eternal vigil against danger—and this may come from any direction. For example, the eyes of the American woodcock have all-round vision of 360 degrees and can sweep the horizon at a glance, but something less than this is more usual for birds.

Hunting species, whether insectivorous swallows, nightjars or raptorous eagles and owls, use vision for locating their next meal, and to be successful they need to be able to judge distances accurately and know just how far to pounce. For this purpose the eyes have come to occupy a more forward-facing position on the head, so that a part of the visual field is scanned by both eyes; overlapping of sight or binocular vision is one method of judging distance, and the degree to which it is developed varies from species to species. All birds, apart from penguins of the genus *Spheniscus*, have some degree of overlapping vision. In pigeons it is only 20 degrees out of their 340-degree angle of vision. By comparison, we have a 140-degree binocular field out of a total visual field of 180 degrees. Owls probably have the most frontally situated eyes of all birds, and the effect is heightened by the fact that their bills, unlike those of other raptors, are deflected downwards more or less to clear their field of

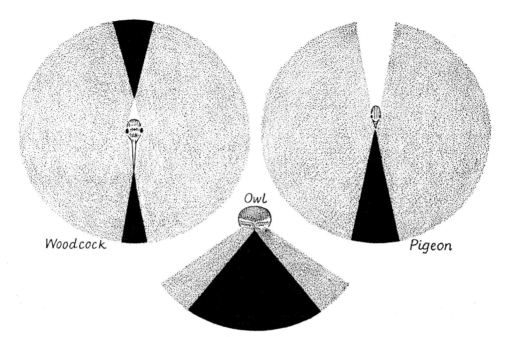

Diagrams showing binocular vision (black) in owls and other species. Their complete range of vision is shaded. Owls, with their forward facing eyes, have the greatest area of three-dimensional (binocular) vision, 70° out of a total field of view of 110°, against the woodcock's 360°.

vision. They have a rather narrow visual field of 110 degrees, of which about 70 degrees is covered by both eyes, so that their three-dimensional visual sense is very well developed, covering two-thirds or more of their field of view. Three-dimensional sight, or stereoscopic vision, is dependent upon the difference between the view of the same area as seen through each eye. The farther apart the eyes are, the better the three-dimensional effect; the closer they are, the more similar the viewpoints of each eye and the less the stereoscopic illusion. It may be no accident, therefore, that the smaller species of owls seem to have squat, flattened heads with eyes placed as far apart as possible, since this compensates for the disadvantage of their scaled-down size in judging distances.

Owls are by no means unique in also using the *parallax* method in judging distances. This involves their bobbing and pivoting in a most attractive manner in order to get several viewpoints of an

Little owl assessing distance by bobbing and turning its head

object, and to observe the relative movement of things within the visual field of vision as the head shifts around. It is easy to understand the value of this method of judging distances if we cover up one eye; the world then suddenly goes flat, like a photograph, but depth of vision is restored if we move our viewpoint around.

One suspects that many people, in attempting to attribute supernatural powers to night owls, forget that eyes are *light receptors*, and that the generously proportioned ones of owls are no exception. Through his poetic licence, Joel Peters has immortalised a popular misconception in his lines from 'The Birds of Wisdom':

> Embodied silence, velvet soft, the owl slips through the night,
> With Wisdom's eyes, Athena's bird turns darkness into light.

Even with 'Wisdom's eyes', nocturnal owls cannot see in the dark, and are as blind as we would be in absolute darkness. However, total darkness is rare in nature and confined to places like deep cave systems where only bats, oilbirds, some fish and a host of invertebrate animals have penetrated. The truth of the matter is that owls are particularly well equipped to make use of whatever light is available, and can detect and approach objects in conditions of illumination that we would subjectively think of as pitch blackness. Moonless, cloudy nights may look very dark to us but the level of illumination rarely drops even then to below 0.004 foot candles. However, experiments have revealed that tawny, Ural, and long-eared owls are able to see and approach prey from a distance of 20ft(6m) when

Barn owl bringing a common shrew to the nest (*Donald A. Smith/Aquila Photographics*)

the illumination is as low as 0.00000016 foot candles. These owls at least would therefore have no difficulty in sighting small rodents at night in a dark forest when it is a comparatively bright 0.0000004 foot candles. Under these circumstances we and indeed some of the owls with less sensitive vision like Tengmalm's and pigmy owls would be blind.

A thorough study of the visual capability of barn owls was made nearly twenty years ago by a postgraduate student, William Curtis, at Cornell University. The method was basically simple, and safeguards were taken to ensure that the results were not due to chance or to the owls' ability to predict the set-up. All the tests took place in a barn loft with a floor area of 20 × 30ft (6 × 9m), and involved the birds flying from one perch to another. Barriers, in the form of white cardboard strips 2in(5cm) wide, were hung from the roof at 5ft(1.5m) intervals midway between the perches and could be moved from time to time so that the owls could not learn to take a particular flight path between them irrespective of whether they could see the strips or not. The barriers were illuminated at different intensities and the behaviour of the owls during their flights, such as whether they collided with the barriers or not, was recorded. So sensitive was the barn owls' night vision that, at first, moonlight seeping through chinks in the walls and roof gave enough light for them to steer clear of the obstructions. The tests were then carried out on dark, cloudy nights but, even so, the light levels at which

(*overleaf*) A variety of species of owls (*Robert Gillmor*)

1 The great gray owl, *Strix nebulosa*, is principally a forest owl. Although it is the largest owl—its size is variously given as 24–33in (61–84cm) and 27in (69cm)—it is not the heaviest.

2 The screech owl, *Otus asio*, 8½in (22cm), has prominent ear tufts, and has grey (left) and red (right) phases. Strictly nocturnal, it occupies a wide range of habitats. The male and female sing in duets.

3 The elf owl, *Micrathene whitineyi*, one of the smallest owls, is only 5¾in (15cm) high. Strictly nocturnal, it roosts and nests in old woodpecker holes in saguaro cactus and trees.

4 The barn owl, *Tyto alba*, has a widespread worldwide distribution. It is 16in (41cm) high and is the only member of the family Tytonidae. Both diurnal and nocturnal, it is probably the most common owl in the world.

5 The burrowing owl, *Athene cunicularia*, 9½in (24cm) high, is a ground dweller, commonly nesting in small colonies in open country—often in prairie dog 'towns'. Its alarm call imitates the rattlesnake.

6 The snowy owl, *Nyctea scandiaca*, 20–27in (51–68.5cm) high is migratory and irruptive. It occupies open tundra, where it hunts by day through the Arctic summer. The juvenile plumage is heavily barred; the male is paler than the female.

(*right*) Little owl with woodmouse prey, often seen at dusk but also during daylight hours (*W. Curtain/Adrea London*)

these owls could operate were so low that Curtis himself was unable to see anything inside the barn, even when his eyes had become dark adapted. Curtis measured the surface brilliance in terms of millilamberts (1 foot candle is equivalent to 1.076 millilamberts) and found that barn owls' vision was sensitive enough to permit identification of the barriers with a brightness of 2×10^{-8} (ie, 0.00000002) millilamberts from a distance sufficient to allow for avoidance.

Next, the illumination was further decreased, whereupon the proportion of collisions in the trials increased until, at a brightness of 2×10^{-9} millilamberts, there was no evidence of the owls being able to see at all; they crashed into the barriers on every trial and became reluctant to fly again that night. The lowest level of illumination which was at all effective in bringing about an adjustment to the direction of flight, preventing the owls coming up against one of the barriers, was 3×10^{-9} millilamberts. This is clearly the visual barrier for barn owls, and their inability to avoid obstacles under conditions of less light indicates beyond doubt that they rely upon no other mysterious sense for their powers of dodging and weaving between the branches of their woodland and scrub habitats. With a visual sensitivity *at least* 35 and probably 100 times better than our own (our lowest threshold may be from 10^{-6} to 1.5×10^{-7} millilamberts), owls would obviously have no difficulty in discerning detail in conditions that would leave us helpless, and to them even a cloudy night might appear no worse than a rather overcast day does to us.

Just why owls' eyes are able to function at light values far below those which our own eyes require is explained in Appendix 1.

The owl's sense of hearing is no less remarkable than its exceptional sight and the two work in conjunction to assist these birds in penetrating darkness. Most birds have ear openings situated just behind the eyes and covered by the head plumage. Projecting pinnae, so characteristic of mammals, are not found in birds because external ear-trumpets would tend to cause too much air resistance in flight. The ear tufts which sit perkily upon the heads of many owl species are nothing to do with their ears; they are merely elongated head feathers and their significance will be discussed in Chapter 2.

Tawny owl at the moment of truth; owls have plumage adapted to silent flight (*Werner Curth/Ardea London*)

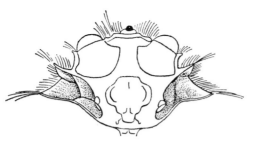

Horizontal section through the head of long-eared owl to show the way the eyes and ears are packed into the skull. (After Schwartzkopff 1962)

Ear flap of long-eared owl

In comparison with other birds, however, the specially nocturnal species of owls like the tawny, barn, long-eared and Tengmalm's and their kin, do have enormously developed ear openings concealed behind the edges of the facial discs. Superficially, these look like concave dishes and it is tempting to suggest that they act like parabolic reflectors to collect sound waves and funnel them down the ear openings. In practice, this seems most unlikely because the position of the external ear openings would seem to be well removed from the focus point, which must be well in front of the owl's face. Yet the harriers, members of the hawk family which hunt by hearing as well as sight, also have rudimentary facial discs, so the two features do seem to be correlated.

If the head of a long-eared owl is examined and the feathers carefully parted, semi-lunar, external ear openings will be found skirting the outer borders of the face, stretching from the top of the skull and running down behind the eyes and corners of the gape, to points on either side of the lower jaw; they all but girdle the head. Furthermore, there are even a series of flaps, or opercula, fringed by stiff feathers, situated to the front and rear of these openings, and it seems that the front one is particularly mobile. So much so that the shape of the ear aperture can be changed at will, and dozing owls can often be seen to erect or depress the plumage on the edge of their facial discs, indicating that their very alert ears are scanning the environment. When the operculum is raised, it is thought that the sense of hearing is directed *behind* the head (ie, rather like a cupped hand held in front of the ear), so in a way the owl may be able to hear well in all directions. The paraphernalia associated with the external ear would alone lead one to the conclusion that their sense of hearing is highly developed, and investigation of the structure of the inner ear and those parts of the brain which interpret the information from it adds further confirmation. (See Appendix 1.)

The fact that these exceedingly efficient sound receivers are also tuned in to high-pitched notes has an important bearing upon an owl's success in catching its prey. Ears, and the way they are tuned, are modified to pick up sounds that have survival value, and the importance of particular sounds will vary from species to species. Owls are great rodent hunters, and voles and mice, as well as rats, have high-pitched squeaky voices, and not very loud ones at that. Furthermore, furtive little rodents scurrying around the hedgerows and dodging beneath twigs and leaves on the forest floor occasionally patter across dried and decaying vegetation, and this might provide a hungry owl with its only clue as to their whereabouts. Noises of this kind contain a great number of high frequencies, and owls are well equipped to react to them. Perhaps most remarkable of all is the fact that barn owls, and probably other kinds with a similarly high degree of ear development, are successful in catching living prey even in *absolute darkness* providing the mouse squeaks or rustles a leaf to give the bird a clue as to where it is. Indeed, so efficient are owls in this respect that they can home in to their prey on a flight trajectory that is accurate to within 1 degree, using their *ears* alone.

Roger Payne, formerly of Cornell University, New York, performed some neat experiments to see just how important as direction-giving clues were the high frequencies emitted by the prey. Barn owls were kept in a room 12ft by 42ft(3.6 × 12.7m) and 6–8ft(1.8–2.4m) high, and on the floor was placed a loud-speaker broadcasting leaf rustles. This cut out as soon as the owl left its perch, and so the bird had to pin-point where the sound came from before it started flying. The room was completely darkened. Normally the flight path or subsequent strike was accurate to within 1 degree, but the accuracy was reduced to between 5 and 7 degrees when frequencies above 8.5 Kh were filtered out. If all the frequencies beyond 5 Kh were removed, the owls refused to strike. Clearly, from sounds of below 5 Kh not enough directional clues could be

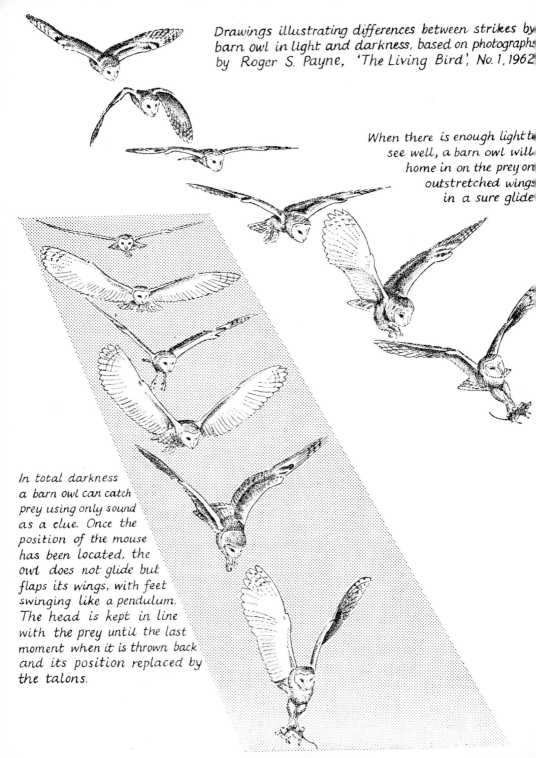

Drawings illustrating differences between strikes by barn owl in light and darkness, based on photographs by Roger S. Payne, 'The Living Bird', No. 1, 1962

When there is enough light to see well, a barn owl will home in on the prey on outstretched wings in a sure glide

In total darkness a barn owl can catch prey using only sound as a clue. Once the position of the mouse has been located, the owl does not glide but flaps its wings, with feet swinging like a pendulum. The head is kept in line with the prey until the last moment when it is thrown back and its position replaced by the talons.

gleaned by their ears to give the owls a sporting chance of success in their strike.

How can sound be used to yield information about direction, and what is so special about the sensitivity of owls' ears that they can be used to intercept prey so accurately? One method relies upon the fact that when the source of noise is to one side of the head, then the sound waves reach one ear before the other. The breadth of an owl's head facilitates this method, since the ear openings are far enough apart to create a sufficient time difference between the arrival of sounds in each ear. This may reach a value of 0.000,03 seconds in both humans and owls, and a time lapse of this degree is sufficient to indicate whether a noise was made to the right or left. Another method depends upon the fact that the head can form a 'sound shadow' on the leeward side of the sound source; in other words, the sound is only perceived clearly in the ear nearest to the trans-mitter. This, however, applies only to those sounds whose wavelength corresponds closely to that of the head width or, less; sounds of longer wavelength tend to fill in behind the head. Sound equivalent to 5 Kh has a wavelength of about 1¾in(44mm), which is approxi-mately the skull width of a barn owl. Species with larger heads (like man) can usually extract information from lower frequency sounds using this method.

But there is probably more to sound location in the barn owl (and no doubt in other large-eared species) than the above explanation alone. An owl flying in to the kill has to make allowance for the fact that its talons are following a different trajectory from that of its head; they are hanging below the body and correspondingly displaced from the line that joins the head and the prey. When there is sufficient light for a barn owl to see its prey, the bird launches itself into the air and makes for the rodent in one decisive glide; but just before striking the wings are raised, the head thrown back, and the feet, with the razor-sharp talons outstretched, are projected forwards. When striking in total darkness the behaviour of the owl differs, as has been demonstrated with the aid of infra-red photo-graphy. When the mouse first rustles some leaves, the owl turns its head towards the prey and, once orientated like this, it must hear one more sound before striking. If it does receive another sound clue, the flight towards the mouse is not a quick sure glide, but the bird flaps vigorously with the feet swinging underneath the body

Short-eared owls are active in daytime (*R.T. Mills/Aquila Photographics*)

like a pendulum. When it has arrived over the prey, again the head is thrown back and the feet swept forwards into the same path as the head was taking a moment before. So when barn owls are flying 'blind', it is the head which is flying on a collision course with the prey, and not until the last moment are the weapons substituted for the sound-detectors.

Another characteristic of the majority of owls, and one which has frightened people out of their wits after dark, is the ability of these birds to appear and disappear like apparitions. Whereas most birds ride the air on whirring noisy wings, owls make their way in and out of shadows in utter silence. Even a 6lb(2.7kg) eagle owl flies with hardly a whisper on its 5ft(1.5m) wing span. It is not difficult to appreciate the survival value for owls of silent flight. First, to a hunter that surprises its victims by pouncing out of the darkness, noisy whistling wings would shatter the silence of the night and give the prey warning of impending attack. Although many nocturnal rodents have miserable sight, their powers of hearing adequately make up for it. Secondly, as owls use sound clues to detect and to home in on their prey, swishing wings would hardly aid their powers of discrimination; in other words, they would deafen themselves to the squeaks and rustles of their prey.

Owls achieve their noiseless flight in two ways. They are endowed with generously proportioned wings so that their weight is spread over, and supported by, relatively large surface areas when they are flying. Although their portly shape might lead one to the conclusion that they are heavy, their loose plumage, in fact, covers comparatively small bodies. A barn owl weighing 505 grammes (one ounce is equivalent to 26 grammes) has a wing area of about 1,680 sq cm (ie, about 1lb supported on an area equivalent to three foolscap sheets of paper), which means that the wing loading is only about 1g for every 3.4sq cm. By comparison, the common crow of North America has a similar weight to that of the barn owl but has a wing loading of 1g/2.4sq cm. The higher the wing loading the more difficult it is for the bird to support itself in the air and the more noise the hard-working wings are likely to make (consider the fuss a heavy, round-winged pheasant makes as it explodes from the undergrowth!). Owls with their low wing loadings glide easily and can fly leisurely through woodlands, or quarter the ground at compara-

Owls are equipped with many sophisticated senses for prey detection and capture

"Ear" tufts express mood and act as nightime recognition signals

Sensitive ears tuned into prey

Large sensitive eyes with binocular vision

Broad wings for manoeuvrability with "silenced" feathers

Strong hooked bill for grasping and tearing prey

Plumage camouflaged for daytime concealment

Widely spread talons, powerful weapons for hitting and gripping the prey. Their wide coverage allows for movement of the prey

Wing feather of tawny owl showing the fine fringes and velvety pile over the surface of the feather which deadens the noise as it beats through the air

tively low speeds. Low wing loading leads to buoyant flight, and this has an even greater survival value for short-eared owls of open spaces, which can actually outclimb a swift-flying peregrine falcon. Incidentally, the migratory owls, like the short-eared and long-eared, have relatively longer wings then sedentary species, and this no doubt helps them in their long journeys. Also, forest-inhabiting owls, like their raptor counterparts, have comparatively short rounded wings to aid manoeuvrability, an important asset in habitats criss-crossed by twigs and branches.

The second adaptation towards achieving quiet flight concerns the structure of the feathers, particularly of the long primary pinions. In most birds whose lives are not dominated by the need for silence, the pinions are usually stiff and resilient, and cut through the air like a knife. Those of typically nocturnal owls, by contrast, are finely fringed at their edges and have a velvet pile on their surfaces. The fine combs are obviously concerned with minimising the noise that wings normally make when they beat through the air, presumably by damping down the movement of air rushing around the surface of the aerofoils. The damping may use up some energy, but this is well spent. The more strictly diurnal hawk, pigmy and fishing owls have hard plumage and, not surprisingly, make more noise on the wing.

The popularity of the owl then stems from its design for coping with, and hunting in, the darkness. Enormous frontal eyes stare out from cheek-like facial discs, and they have wide, almost bulbous, heads like ours for accommodating the widely spaced and highly developed ears; both are part of the owl's equipment for homing in on elusive and alert prey. The tools of a killer, although of mesmeric quality, to us are never particularly endearing. The owl, however, misleads us because the tools of his trade are neatly concealed—as near as birds will ever produce to the wolf in sheep's clothing. Soft, billowing plumage fills the body out into a cuddly, round shape, hiding cruel, savage talons and a decurved predatory beak which, incidentally, pokes out just where we would expect a nose to be! Add to this a seemingly elastic neck and cute ear tufts, and here is a bird which is a caricature of man. Athene's bird might not be able to work the miracle of turning night into day, but the truth in the case of owls turns out to be no less remarkable.

2 *Owls at Home*

Animals tend to spend their time in more or less fixed areas or territories. These are places where the layout of the land is familiar, so giving the individual a feeling of security. Somewhere within the home-range is usually a base, which may act as a resting, roosting, or nesting site.

Home, to an owl, is very often a crevice or natural cavity, or a branch hidden by thick foliage, where the day can be spent asleep and the spoils of the previous night's hunting digested. Some owls even roost on the ground, such as short-eared and snowy owls, both being species found in exposed places where tree cover may be sparse, if not absent. Sleeping places may be occupied for long periods, and some idea of the duration of tenure may be afforded by the accumulation of pellets which often cover the area beneath the roost, and can be several feet thick. Tawny owls regularly change their roosts, and the short-eared owl, which usually favours grass tussocks, may never roost twice in the same place.

By day, when other birds are alert to danger, the sleeping owl must replace vigilance with other tactics if it is to survive. Roosting sites are, therefore, chosen for their safety—because a dozing owl is a vulnerable owl, with its senses partially dimmed by the need to sleep—with the equally important consideration of affording shelter from the weather. It is perhaps a strange twist of fate that one of the owl's natural enemies, apart from starvation, is another owl. Barn, barred, long-eared, and screech owls all appear on the menu of the great horned owl. Similarly, in Europe, the eagle owl is by no means averse to taking any owl so unwary as to let these fine killers come too close. Tawny owls, too, have certainly been known to prey upon the introduced little owl in Great Britain. Luckily, owls all tend to be asleep at the same time, and so are not threatened at their roosts by bigger and bolder relatives to any appreciable extent. There are, too, a host of carnivorous, tree-climbing mammals, and diurnal birds of prey which would not hesitate at the chance of taking an owl for food, and it is predation pressures of this sort which have forced owls to take care in choosing where to close their eyes and bury their heads in their soft scapular feathers. Tawny owls usually roost high up in trees, often taking shelter behind ivy, and their tendency to change their sleeping quarters frequently might possibly be an inborn strategy designed to keep them one jump ahead of their enemies.

Although owls could not be described as sociable birds, several species do show a loose kind of gregariousness in their roosting habits. There are several accounts of barn owls coming together to sleep; as many as fifty have been flushed from a clump of oaks in the USA, and once fourteen were counted leaving a roost in an old tree. Cross timbers in bridges are reputed to be favourite haunts for roosting barn owls. Short-eared and long-eared owls also tend to form communal roosts; again, fifty of the latter species have been counted in one thicket. Of course, it is possible that during the winter owl families might tend to keep together, and when several owls are flushed from a roost they may be a pair and their surviving offspring.

While the social sleeping habits of owls pale into insignificance when compared to the communal dusk gatherings of birds like starlings or gulls, there is a question as to why some owls do tend to sleep in close proximity to others of their kind. Perhaps certain spots are more favourable as daytime retreats than others, and so owls in the neighbouring areas may tend to flight in towards them as the eastern sky lights up. In other words, basically asocial owls congregate in the few desirable sleeping quarters. The same phenomenon occurs with pill bugs—terrestrial crustaceans—which accumulate beneath damp, cool stones, not because they enjoy each other's company but because a combination of conditions that ensure their survival 'turns off' the animals' exploratory or 'seeking' drive.

It is also possible that the coming together of long-eared and barn owls into roosts is more than a passive accumulation in specifically favourable sites. Perhaps these birds, and a few other kinds which from time to time show this behaviour, are genuinely sociable when off duty, and the purpose of these gatherings has some kind of

communication value. Pied wagtails, for instance, are more or less solitary hunters by day, but at night they come together, often in hundreds, to sleep in reed beds, or even in the warm, lush environment of commercial greenhouses.

However, between species, owls often act with great animosity towards each other. Indeed, sometimes an owl's deadliest enemy may well be another larger bird of prey. Eagle owls and goshawks are especially murderous, and can account for 90% of recorded owl deaths in parts of Northern Europe where several raptors and owls share the countryside. Not surprisingly, eagle owls are at the top of the pecking order because of their size, and they have been known to predate even upon powerful, speedy birds like peregrines. Strife can be particularly lethal between tawny and Ural owls which tend to compete head on for similar nest sites. When fighting breaks out, the Urals are dominant, and can annihilate the less pugnacious tawnies.

It is therefore no wonder that owls need to conceal themselves from the world. The first prerequisite for security is camouflage, and owls certainly excel themselves in being able to blend into the background. And, since concealment is less necessary to nocturnal hunting, it can be deduced that the owl's beautifully cryptic plumage has been evolved as a result of its need to remain hidden by day. Of course, there are exceptions. High Arctic species may have to hunt by the light of the sun, and so camouflage is as necessary for them, if they are not to forewarn their prey, as it is for their daytime counterparts, the hawks. White and black spangled, the colouring of the snowy owl is just right for concealing these big birds against the broken snowscape. Curiously enough, some of the cocks are almost pure white, whereas their larger mates tend to have more barred grey or white plumage.

The pattern and general coloration of the feathers have, of course, evolved in relation to certain features of the more usual home areas. The snowy owl is a good example; when these birds nest well south of their normal range, in the Shetlands for instance, their white plumage looks curiously out of place and renders the birds highly conspicuous, although it does not seem to put them at a disadvantage in catching their food. Great gray or Lapland owls are able to 'vanish' in the weeping, mossy treescapes of the taiga forests. Desert

Great Gray or Lapland owl, *Strix nebulosa* (*Göran Hanssonn*)

owls tend to be paler, and more yellow, than their forest cousins, while those of tropical rain forests, such as the *Ciccaba* (wood) and *Pulsatrix* (spectacled) owls, are very dark brown in general colouring. Prettiest of all the owls must be the Asian bay owls with their richly patterned plumage of greys, chestnuts, and warm brown and buff.

Various principles may be adopted by animals to aid their conceal-ment. One of these involves countershading, whereby highlights and shadows formed by predominantly unidirectional lighting, usually from above, are nullified by differential shading in the plumage. So it is that most birds are darker above than below, thus rendering them 'flat' and, therefore, unreal when illuminated from above, a valuable trick of colouring because hunters are looking for three-dimensional prey. Owls are predominantly upright birds that inhabit relatively dark places with suffused light. Since shadow function is reduced, many woodland owls tend not to be countershaded; if they are so shaded, the paler areas of the plumage tend to be in the belly and lower chest regions where a shadow would be formed by their 'vertical' bodies. Owls which expose themselves to the sunlight, like the burrowing and short-eared owls, tend to be more countershaded than others.

Illusions are also created by obliterative markings, which are employed to 'break up' the body. The burrowing owl has strong transverse bars running across the chin, and it is possible that the white V-shaped markings formed by the scapular feathers on the backs of certain owls—such as the saw-whet, flammulated, screech and whiskered owls—may also tend to make their owners less recognisable to the searching eyes of their enemies. In general, however, the owl's camouflage depends upon its similarity to the background. Dappled light thrown on to the branches by foliage is mimicked by the colouring of many species. The vertical striations on the underparts of long-eared owls must match the striated bark of coniferous trees in which they roost, and lichen-covered trunks form a background into which many woodland owls effectively melt.

Some types of owls are *dimorphic*, that is to say the adults occur in two basic colour varieties. Many of the screech and scops owls have 'brown' and 'red' phases, and these often live side by side. The tawny owl has a rarer 'grey' phase. It is possible that both varieties of dimorphic species have survival value, but each comes into its own in different habitats, if the species' choice of habitat is catholic. Whatever the reason, there is little doubt that no *one* form is better than the other, so the two colour phases reach a balanced level within some owl populations.

The best and most perfect of camouflages would, however, be rendered useless if it were not used properly. Movement always attracts attention and roosting owls only remain hidden if they keep still. Behaviour, therefore, is no less important than the incredibly cryptic colouring that has been developed. Those who have discovered a roosting owl might be tempted to go along with the sentiment expressed about the wise old owl who lived in an oak, 'the more he

The white-faced scops owl nests in trees of the African savannah (*Michael Gore/Nature Photographers Ltd*)

Dimorphism in screech owl,
(bird on left in alert posture)

Grey phase   Brown phase

saw the less he spoke'. Looking disdainfully down through the canopy, with only an occasional wink of an eye, the owl is following an inherited response of remaining as still as possible when prowlers are around, and giving his covering of brown or grey spangled feathers a chance to do their job properly. Although the naturalist can probably find roosting owls more easily than someone with an unpractised eye, the owl on his daytime perch is putting his trust in an automatic strategy for survival—and more often than not is rewarded by the earthbound disturber of the day's sojourn walking

Short-eared owls nest on the ground, hidden amongst long grass or bushes
(*N.W. Harwood/Aquila Photographics*)

away. The owl sees all without being seen, whereas jumping around in an agitated fashion would immediately have given the game away. Ironically enough, the owl's tactics of doing practically nothing unless danger is acute has been mistaken by folk over the ages for cleverness and intellect, whereas an animal like the hedgehog, for instance, which does essentially the same thing, rolling up into a ball to allow the covering of spines to deter the enemy, is regarded as stupid. This is partly because one of the hedgehog's chief adversaries today is the motor car, in the face of which the mammal's form of defence, effective though it is against foxes and the like, proves singularly inappropriate.

Long-eared owls adopt a special posture when frightened at their roosts. While asleep, the owls may fluff themselves out to improve the insulating properties of the plumage. But should danger threaten, the owl presses the plumage to the body and stretches upwards, ear tufts erect, thereby assuming a long, thin posture. The owl then looks more like a broken-off stub, not at all the sort of shape a predator would associate with a tasty meal.

Owls that roost in the open are often bedevilled by persistent mobbing attacks from smaller birds. If a foraging great tit unexpectedly comes across a tawny or long-eared owl, it will keep its distance and exhibit alarm movements of the wings and tail, at the same time uttering very characteristic calls. As likely as not, these will attract a host of other small birds, and they will all mob the owl together. Mobbing is the common response of birds to certain predators that pose some degree of threat—for example, mammalian hunters such as cats, foxes and snakes, from which birds with their ability to fly have more than a sporting chance of escape, providing they are not caught unawares. Presumably this behaviour has survival value to the mobbers by drawing everyone's attention to the whereabouts of the killer. The participants make themselves conspicuous with wing and tail cocking movements, and their alarm calls are usually raucous and repetitive with a wide frequency range to offer as many directional clues to all birds within earshot.

This situation contrasts strongly with the response by small birds to very dangerous aerial predators, such as peregrines or sparrowhawks; these elicit alarm reactions of quite a different sort, such as fleeing to the nearest cover and freezing. The calls given are usually thin and high-pitched, and are drawn out with no real beginning or ending, so that it is difficult to locate the whereabouts of the caller; in fact, they have a ventriloquial quality. Alarm is thus signalled to all within hearing distance without the signaller betraying his own location, an obvious advantage if the enemy is fast and can fly! It is perhaps curious that owls are neither treated with indifference nor as other birds of prey, and the fact that they, together with crows and jays for example, are mobbed, indicates that owls must be treated warily by small birds, and rightly, as pellet analysis shows. We can hazard a guess that although resting owls pose little threat to birds in general, some owls are diurnal and more dangerous than others, so that birds cannot afford to take chances. Yet, in fact, owls are not as potentially dangerous to other birds as hawks. When owls are around, and have been discovered, the action which best ensures survival of the local birds seems to lie in exposing the enemy by means of mass displaying. After all, surprise is a predator's chief ally, and to small birds an exposed predator is a 'paper tiger'.

Experiments have shown that owls are recognised by their characteristic rounded shape, and that in song sparrows at least, the response to owls is inborn, that is to say no learning is involved. In chaffinches, hawfinches, reed buntings, and yellowhammers, the mobbing response does not appear until they are several weeks old, but then occurs automatically as a result of a nervous maturation or growth process, without needing any experience of owls. Furthermore, when stylised owl shapes are placed in aviaries the amount of mobbing tends to wane with each presentation. In the artificial conditions of captivity, successive introductions may even result in a long-term reduction of the mobbing response, so that the model, or even a stuffed owl, eventually becomes accepted as part and parcel of the surroundings. Under natural circumstances one suspects that this would not happen, although a short-term waning of the mobbing response probably does occur, or else owls would be unmercifully harassed throughout their 'sleeping life'. Although owls will occasionally attempt to escape from a troop of 'clacking' and 'chinking' birds, they are more likely to do nothing. The mobbers then lose interest. Experiments have shown that once birds have 'mobbed' in one place, they will either avoid the area or exhibit alarm reactions, perhaps months after, at the spot where the owl was encountered. An owl's roost, once

Boreal owl being mobbed by small birds

discovered, might therefore tend to be avoided by birds which have taken part in the mobbing, although should the owl change its sleeping place it will probably have to put up with further mobbing by the local bird population.

Hunters have made use of the inborn reaction of birds to owls. In his fine book *Hunting*, Gunnar Brusewitz has outlined methods whereby owls have been employed to lure wary species within range of guns and nets. Eagle owls have always been a favourite with hunters, and countless thousands, if not millions, of crows, jays and magpies have met their end from a far more devious enemy than the one on which their attention had been riveted. So effective is this method that there is one report of as many as 120 jays being caught during a single day. Smaller birds could also be lured for the pot by using an owl decoy, and these were often caught by cleft sticks or bird lime. If the hunting was good, then the perches round the owl would have to be cleared and relimed several times a day. But owls were not always used to entice birds to their death; an eagle owl with a fox's brush tethered to it, to make it more conspicuous, was an indispensable part of the team for hunting buoyant-winged kites. Only when these fine birds of prey were busy mobbing the owl at a low altitude were the speedy peregrines or lanners loosed. The aim was to ground the kite, and afterwards it was released. Sometimes, however, the hawks or falcons did not return to the fist, and the falconers, always eager to make good their losses, snared goshawks in nets while they made parries at a jessed and tethered owl. Today, the technique has been brought up to date by bird photographers interested in snapping the hosts of angry, mobbing birds that are aroused by a tethered owl placed near their nests or feeding areas.

In North America, the old bird-catching techniques have come in useful for capturing birds of prey for ringing (or banding as it is known in the United States). Thus, a great horned owl tethered beneath a nest has been successfully employed for catching hen harriers (or marsh hawks). The apparatus is placed near the harriers' nest, and as the parents stoop on to the trespassing owl, they may collide with the net. When used in this way, more hens are caught than cocks. Even ospreys have been caught by setting up the *dho-gazas*—as they are called—on floating timbers! The advantage of this method is that raptorous birds and even owls, always elusive to bird-banders when they are grown up, can be caught without injury. Snowy and barred owls would probably be suitable as decoys.

Owls are not, on the whole, gregarious. Here we tend to use species like gannets or sandwich terns as a yardstick for comparison because they nest in vast bird cities, but, like so many other seabirds including penguins, auks, gulls, petrels, and so on, they are special cases because they feed over vast areas of the sea by themselves, only coming to land to breed, where their freehold requirements on protected sites are modest. After the breeding season is over, each bird goes its own way, although concentrations of food may tend to draw many individuals together. There is another kind of sociableness, like that exhibited by starlings which flock in the winter after

Bird-catching using cleft sticks and a decoy eagle owl

Bird-catcher making himself into a portable hide, based on a German illustration of 1501

Birds coming to mob a decoy owl become trapped on twigs coated with bird-lime

Hawks readily mob eagle owls and could be caught in fine nets hung close to the decoy

the pairs have spent the summer dispersed in territories; these have had to provide both protection for the nest and a good food supply. Other species, like the village and red-billed weavers, are intensely gregarious all the year round, and this is dictated by the pattern of food dispersal, allowing optimal exploitation, as well as being an anti-predator device operating on the principle of safety in numbers.

As in the case of the weaver birds, food often determines the type of social organisation permitted of animals exploiting it. For example, avian predators—social all, or part of, the year round—are rare in nature, and tend to be confined to some insectivorous kinds whose hunting is not hampered by the presence of other individuals, as with bee-eaters, which often hunt in flocks and breed in colonies. But if success in the kill depends upon stealth, as it does for owls which feed on alert and fast-moving prey, then hunting must be a solitary business conducted in a home range of sufficient size to bear enough food and to ensure a clear field for the hunter. To lead a solitary life, however, is not necessarily to live like a recluse without contact with others of the same kind. Territories, no matter what their size, tend to fit together like the pieces of a jigsaw puzzle, simply because birds of a like prefer to set up home near each other, so forming 'neighbourhoods'. Owls may be lone hunters, but they probably like to live in loose kinds of communities, with neighbours at a safe distance but not too far away.

Community life, whether of the packed spectacular bird-ghetto variety or the spacious 'stockbroker belt' sort characteristic of owls, implies that there are rules for spacing and tenancy, and there must be communication between the members to make the system work smoothly. Owls must sort out the boundaries of their territories; there must be recognition of friends and foes, or of other kinds of owls which pose no threat; mates have to be attracted, and so on. A language has, therefore, been evolved which allows disputes to be settled, and breeding to be carried out with the maximum of ease.

Animal language is, of course, quite different from our own. We can express complicated ideas and concepts, and describe our intentions by means of speech. No other species has this capability under natural circumstances, although chimps have been taught a few simple words. Nevertheless, at the same time we supplement our language with more basic clues as to our motivation, such as facial expressions, body posturing, flushing, and occasionally grunts and screams, and these can denote such emotions as pleasure, anger, appeasement, fear, dominance and so on. All who can see and interpret the 'signals' are thus able to predict the reactions of the displaying individual, and modify their behaviour accordingly. Similarly, the signals of birds can be interpreted; they may have inflexible beaks and fairly fixed faces but they adequately make up for this 'signalling' deficiency by using all the resources of their own bodies to form a language involving wing movements, feather erections, and voice, by means of which adequate information about

Young great horned
owl in defensive
display (*Ardea London*)

the mood and intentions of the signaller can be conveyed to others sharing the same code of behaviour. For each species has its own particular language.

Plumage plays an important role in bird language because either the whole of the body plumage or individual groups of feathers can be erected or depressed at will to bring about startling changes in outline or colour. Such displays can be turned 'on' and 'off' very quickly by the action of the feather papillae muscles, similar to those that make our hair stand on end. Confidence might be communicated by sleek feathering, while a bird with its plumage fluffed out will possibly be a weak, submissive individual advertising the fact that it wants to be left alone. This is a very generalised example to illustrate how the state of the plumage can serve as a clue to the wearer's mood. However, language is usually far more specific, particularly when it comes to the signals that birds use to threaten or woo each other. In such cases the plumage is modified to reinforce their communication function, over and above the more usual requirements for insulation, camouflage and aerodynamics. Over the course of evolution, feathers which are erected during some display or other tend to become changed in such a manner as to add impact to the display, thereby making the feather movements more effective as signals. And these, in consequence, become clearer to interpret by those who see them. In other words, the message must ring, or shine, loud and clear.

The addition of bright colours is one way of making conspicuous the plumage that is raised to reflect some mood or other; for example, the reddish-orange breast feathers of the robin are displayed during sparring matches. Other evolutionary developments involve changes in size and structure of feathers which make their use in displays far more dramatic than normal ones. The peacock's upper tail coverts, or the secondary wing feathers of the Argus pheasant, are perhaps the most bizarre examples of this in the bird world, but 'signalling' feathers have evolved into various other forms such as erectile plumes, beards, capes, and pennants, all of which are found widely distributed among birds. So far as crests or ear tufts are concerned, those of owls can undoubtedly be erected and depressed, and so in all probability these birds' intentions of attack or withdrawal can be communicated to other individuals. More spectacular crests than those of owls are found in the diurnal cockatoos, which often reveal beautiful patterns or colours when they are spread; an example of this is Major Mitchell's cockatoo, with its head fan of crimson and orange feathers. Because of their fore and aft construction, such crests are undoubtedly designed to show off to a neighbour approaching broadside, rather than dead ahead as in the case of the owls. Again, some diurnal birds of prey have elongated head feathers which can be erected to frame the head from the front; these have been called 'fright masks', and certainly some of the hawk eagles appear savage in the extreme when their crests are erected. One of them, the magnificent harpy eagle, even has an 'eared' mask like a giant eagle owl. Exactly what function these masks fulfil is something of a mystery, but some birds of prey certainly do have defensive postures similar to the 'sun fan' displays of owls, which are discussed later, and the masks may make these postures even more effective.

Apart from signals which need to be turned on and off, such as threat or precopulatory displays, animals also carry around with them species' recognition marks which distinguish them from other kinds of closely related birds. The precise pattern of the plumage may operate as a species' badge, or even the shape and size of the bill, as in the Galapagos finches, all of which have evolved their own specialised feeding equipment and therefore have quite characteristic profiles. Often the badges are worn on the wings and shown off to their best advantage when the birds take to flight. Wading birds often have nicely differentiated wing and rump patterns, and dabbling ducks have their metallic coloured specular which have been likened to the simple and stylised patterns of national flags. When they are suddenly disturbed, all birds with similar markings tend to coalesce into a flock, helped by the fact that members of similar species tend to fly at the same speed. Bullfinches, which have white rumps, are able to follow each other while darting in and out of thick cover.

Day birds have light on their side when it comes to displaying, and most owls cannot claim much assistance from the sun when it comes to communicating. For this reason, owl displays are particularly interesting. Whether they be of the instantly turned-on-and-off type, or the permanently switched-on variety, the visual signals of owls must all be capable of functioning by night. To start with, most owls are cryptic and not highly coloured; indeed bright patches of colour would be only of limited use at night, particularly where vision over any distance is impeded by foliage. It is not surprising, then, that long-distance communication is chiefly carried out by voice in owls, and visual displays mainly kept for short-distance signalling between birds confronting each other, perhaps on the same branch. These displays will be discussed later. Although colours and patterns, reinforced by plumage erections, might not be effective as a system of long-distance signalling at night, distinctive silhouettes combined with voice would be a sure means of species identification. It is, therefore, very interesting that owls do, in fact, have quite characteristic profiles, and in fifty-seven species these are enhanced by the presence of ear tufts. As stated before, these are nothing to do with hearing but merely groups of feathers projecting from the scalp. Since non-eared and eared species often live side by side, the presence or absence of tufts may be a useful guide to owls in helping them to distinguish each other in the field, apart, of course, from their use, already referred to, as short-distance indicators of changing moods.

Ear tufts vary enormously in size from species to species; in the genera *Otus, Bubo, Rhinotynx, Ketupa, Jubula* and *Lophostrix*, they are well developed and project more to the side of the head, like devil's horns. In the genus *Asio*, three kinds of nocturnal and woodland-inhabiting long-eared owls have, as their name suggests, conspicuous tufts sitting vertically on top of the head; in the two predominantly diurnal 'short-eared' *Asio* owls, the tufts are rudimentary. The latter inhabit open country, and it could be concluded that their need for special 'outline' recognition signals might be less than that of their woodland-living relatives.

It is also interesting to compare the visual recognition signals of owls with those of other night-living birds, such as the nightjars. These spend the day squatting on the ground and are hard to find because of their perfectly adapted camouflage, but at night they stir into action, and become insect catchers. Many species have white wing or tail markings that would appear to be signals, either for recognition or for use in courtship situations, or both. North American nighthawks and pauraques have species-characteristic white markings on their otherwise black wing feathers, just where national roundel markings would be placed on aircraft. Others, like the whip-poor-will, have partially white outer tail feathers. Sexual recognition is also made possible by distinctive markings, as well as through the voice. The cock European nightjar has white spots on its wings which draw attention to its wing movements while it is courting, and two African nightjars have adopted a silhouette form of sexual recognition. Both the standard and pennant-winged nightjars have long, trailing, primary wing feathers, one on each wing, and recent observations of the latter species in Nigeria have shown how the cocks use their strange 'standards' for courtship. When displaying in front of a hen, the cock flies around her on stiff, vibrating wings, with the pennants held vertically above like two small satellites. The advantage of distinctive silhouettes like these as a means of signalling at night is obvious.

It is possible that visual signals are more appropriate to the nightjars and their kin because they spend more time on the wing hunting over reasonably open ground than most owls do. Like owls, however, nightjars are more often heard than seen, and many have almost interminable and repetitious songs, from which they get their names; for example, 'whip-poor-will' and 'chuck-will's widow' are onomatopaeic renderings of their songs. The European nightjar's song is a simple 'churr', alas now becoming rather rare in parts of the British Isles where heathland is becoming developed or ploughed up.

Owls are very vociferous and doubtless species recognition is as much effected through vocal as visual means; their hoots and screams make up a well-developed language. Owls are not song birds, and yet the clear hooting of tawny owls answering each other over wooded valleys, perhaps punctuated by the barking of dog foxes, is as pleasing to the ear as any chorus of nightingales or blackbirds. In Europe, it is certainly an evocative sound of the night, and countless records must have been worn down by drama producers in radio, television, and in the theatre attempting to conjure up the night atmosphere for their audience. Equally, thoughts of the warm, balmy nights of the Mediterranean, heavy with the smell of lime and citrus blossom, can be aroused by the 'chimes' of the scops owl. Although we tend to refer to the calls of the owls as 'hoots', some make quite strange noises which could be described as growls, snores, buzzes, screeches and coughs. The calls of the midwife toad could be

WHIP-POOR-WILL
North America

STANDARD-WINGED NIGHTJAR
Africa

NIGHTJAR
Europe

PAURAQUE
Central America

NIGHTHAWK
North America

Some night flying birds
have special markings
or wing feathers to help
recognition in the dark

EAGLE OWL
Europe

TAWNY OWL
Europe & Asia

WHITE-FACED SCOPS OWL
Africa

LONG-EARED OWL
Europe

MALAYSIAN FISH OWL
South East Asia

ELF OWL
Southern Arizona

*Owls have their own
distinctive silhouettes
and these may help
them to recognise
each other at night*

mistaken for the voice of the scops owl; in fact, this very misidenti-
fication takes place on a German natural history record called 'Vogel
stimmen aus Südeuropa' by G. Thielcke and C. König (75–09255).
The North American saw-whet owl has a voice not unlike that of
stridulating grasshopper, and the blood-curdling scream of a woman
in dire distress might not be worth answering in Australia as it could
be a barking owl, which can also growl like a dog. Except in the
case of the really deep-voiced species, the term 'hooting' hardly does
justice to the owl songs of the night, because songs they really are.

Although owl hoots and the sweet warbling of thrushes seem
poles apart, they both serve the same biological ends. Songs are two-
edged weapons; first, they are tools of territorial assertion. A hooting
owl is signalling its right to territorial ownership, and to other cocks
the hoots mean 'keep out, this is my pad'. Hooting, like singing, is
a deeply infectious activity, and neighbouring owls will tend to
answer each other in chorus. On very quiet nights, owls can be
heard responding to each other; as a nearby bird calls, a series of
others, at increasing distances away, can be heard replying, fainter
and fainter, like so many echoes. Thus, within a very short time,
owls in a neighbourhood are able to inform each other of the
whereabouts of their hunting areas. Night after night during the
hooting seasons, usually in autumn and spring, owls get to know
each other, presumably through the minor individual differences in
their songs, and should one fail to join in the chorus, or strike up
only feebly, then his territory will be quickly taken over, probably
in a bloodless battle of hooting and chasing, rather like a war
between choristers. The effect upon vigorous territory-holders of
having an intruding, hooting owl in their neighbourhood may be
judged by any good bird mimic hooting in a wood occupied by
owls. Luckily, this is easy to stage because tawny owls are easily
mimicked. Apart from answering, the chances are that the resident
owls will come to investigate, and may even be tempted to attack.
Saw-whet owls can thus be called up and, according to some
accounts, may even perch on an outstretched arm.

Singing also has a sexual function; as it is chiefly carried out by
the cocks, their hooting during the spring doubtless attracts hens,
and in long established pairs stimulates ovulation, thereby bringing
the hens into breeding condition. The advertising function of hooting

would seem to be illustrated by an account of the activities of snowy owls on Southampton Island in May and June, related by Dr George M. Sutton in *Life Histories of North American Birds of Prey*. He states that on the brightest days the deep booming notes of dozens of snowy owls floated across the rosy-white snow plains, and the air fairly throbbed with dull thick sounds. One morning as many as twenty birds could be counted, probably all cocks. One bird was perched on a boulder and, on calling, it lifted its head, the throat swelling out enormously, elevated its tail vertically and gave vent to four loud hoots, bowing violently each time. The behaviour has every sign of being a long-range visual and acoustic advertising display, with the birds perching on exposed features and performing regularly. Owls sometimes hoot regularly on the wing. The song of the Tengmalm's owl may be emitted as the cock flies closely round the crown of the tree in which the hen is sitting. Wing clapping also plays an important role in this species, although this may be concerned more with territorial acclamations than courtship.

The voices of owls, particularly the larger ones, tend to have a very human-like quality, and this has survival value for them. It is possible to reproduce songs in the form of sound pictures, whereby the different pitches or frequencies at any given moment are spread out rather as light passing through a prism is split up into its constituent colours. These sound pictures are called spectrograms, and analysis of a whole series of owl songs or hoots reveals that there is a relationship between the size of the owl and the basic frequency of the voice. The eagle and great gray owls have deep bass hoots with a frequency range not extending much beyond 1 Kh, whereas the diminutive pigmy owl has a high-pitched call, more of a whistle than a 'hoot', with a frequency range extending from 2 Kh to 8.5 Kh.

Even so, the majority of owls have relatively low-pitched hoots. High-frequency notes have only limited carrying power, and would tend to become dissipated by such barriers as tree trunks, foliage, and the tangle of forest branches. On the other hand, deep bass frequencies have much greater carrying power, rather like foghorns, and since owls need to communicate over some distances, their hoots are nicely adapted to act as sound beacons in the darkness. The diurnal snowy owl's deep booming is reputed to carry at least

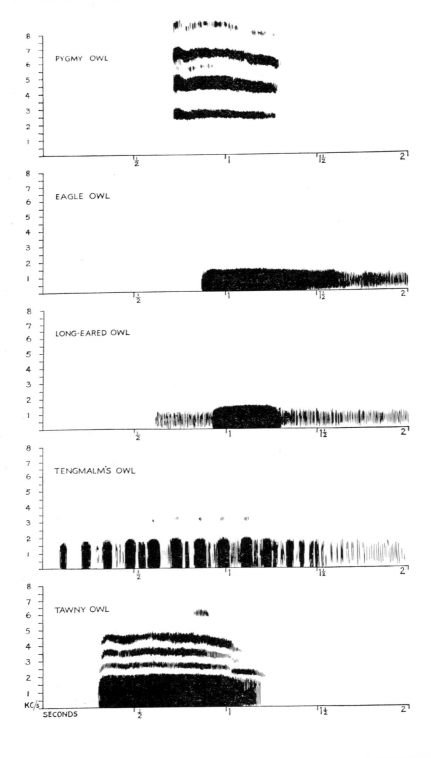

7miles(11km). It is also of interest here to note that owls inhabiting thick woodland areas are, on the whole, much more vocal than open-country owls; compare the noisy tawny with the more or less silent short-eared owl. The snowy owl, however, would appear to be an exception to this general rule.

The structure of the songs is no less interesting. The names of some owls are taken from their calls, such as the screech, morepork, book-book, laughing and barking owls, to name but a few. As field aids to the unmusical, the songs of other owls have been translated into all manner of ditties; for example, it has been written of the screech owl, the common eared owl of North America, that the song is in the form of 'mutual consolations of suicide lovers remembering the pangs and the delights of supernal love in the infernal groves . . . *Oh -o -o -o -o that I had never been bor -r -r -r -r -n*'. The barred owl hoots '*I cook today, you cook tomorrow*', and by some stretch of the imagination, the tremulous song of the tawny has been turned into '*Tu-whit, tu-whoo*'.

There is a rough analogy between the hoots of owls and the Morse code. Each species has its own style of hooting, with 'dots' and 'dashes' being replaced by short and long hoots. There are owls with simple voices like the single, monosyllabic hoots of the eagle and long-eared. Others form phrases by running together a series of hoots; these are long in the case of the great gray and horned owls, and are equivalent to a series of 'dashes' in morse code analogy, or short in the case of the beautiful Tengmalm's owl, where they are equivalent to a run of 'dots'. The song phrases may be repeated several times a minute, in fact twelve to fifteen times for Tengmalm's. Syncopated calls are characteristic of many owls; these phrases include both long drawn out and shorter hoots, for example the tawny, Ural, and barred owls. Since song and voice are specific recognition mechanisms, preventing attempts at hybridisation or cross-breeding between different kinds, owls have presumably been under evolu-

Tawny owl continued

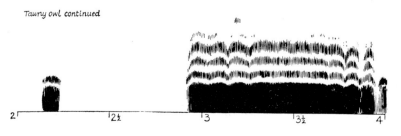

tionary pressures to develop their own characteristic voices. So, without evolving elaborate songs like the song birds, with each species having its own melody, many owls have obtained the same result by ringing the changes on a 'Morse code' principle.

Hooting does not a language make, though, and owls certainly have a language. The repertoire of calls, other than the song, varies from species to species. There are alarm calls, flight calls, and notes which are characteristic of the age and sex of the caller, very important in birds where the sexes are similar in appearance. Begging, anger, and nest invitation can also be communicated by voice. In these cases the calls have to operate at short distances, and are often soft and intimate in tone; so, movements of the throat made when vocalising are very often reinforced by the synchronous exposure of the pale plumage in this region. Owls also snap their mandibles together to produce a rhythmic clicking noise, and this seems to occur in situations where a bird is on the defensive. It is probably a stylised biting movement, and is given as a warning.

Reproduction requires the utmost co-operation and co-ordination between a pair of owls. Both partners are efficient, territorial hunters, selfish by our standards and yet over the course of a few months they will live together harmoniously, decide on a nest site, mate, and share out food to the owlets. All these activities must be performed in an organised manner. Clumsy matings may produce infertile eggs; a hungry incubating bird will as likely as not desert the eggs; a parent incapable of sharing food with its offspring will leave no descendants. The whole business of making a success of breeding is made possible by a system of signals.

Courtship is often a hazardous business, particularly for powerful killers like owls where there is as a rule virtually no apparent difference between the sexes. Since owls are for the most part territorial creatures and will if necessary defend their rights to occupancy by all the means at their disposal, the approach of a mate which, to all intents and purposes, shows the same characteristics as a rival, is a delicate and danger-fraught situation. So far as the cock is concerned, he will be tempted to react in several different ways at the same time. The individual that looks like a hated rival must be attacked and driven from the area; at the same time an urge to mate will conflict with the aggression. Similarly, the hen may be on the one hand frightened and tempted to avoid the bold cock owl, and at the same time tend to hold her ground and let him copulate with her. She may even react by launching an attack on him.

Before mating becomes possible, then, a number of problems have to be overcome. First, there is the difficulty of sex recognition. Hen owls, like most hawks, are usually larger than their mates but, apart from the snowy owl, are otherwise similar. Even in the case of the snowy owl, there is a great deal of variation in the sexes so that the lightest hens are no different from the more mottled cocks. Secondly, the fear of the hen at being approached by the cock has to be subdued and replaced by sexual responses. Thirdly, the killing drive of the hen has to be switched off, because the weapons at her disposal would be very damaging if they were turned against every potential mate. It seems likely that in owls, as in other birds where cocks and hens look alike, recognition of potential mates lies in behaviour. Unmated hen and cock owls would react quite differently to the overtures of an unattached, territory-holding cock. The hen would probably act in a conciliatory manner, whereas the wandering cock on the lookout for both mate and territory would either flee or stay and fight. A cock owl on the lookout for a mate is therefore keenly interested in a stranger's responses, because these will give him initially the chief clue as to whether it is a potential partner or a rival.

Further clues are provided by the voice; hens tend to answer the hooting of the cocks with their own distinctive calls. For example, the quavering, syncopated hooting of a cock tawny owl is often answered with a 'kee-wick' from a hen, probably his mate. Sometimes, as in tawny and barred owls, this is a kind of 'ragged' responsiveness, whereas in others it is strictly antiphonal singing; that is, two birds contributing to form a single well-organised song. Spectacled owls answer each other with perfect regularity as if 'they were striking the heads of different-sized barrels with wooden mallets'. Eagle and little owls also duet. Duetting has been recorded in many other birds, and tends to be correlated with dense habitats where the sexes may have difficulty in keeping in sight of each other. Voice, therefore, acts as a kind of 'lifeline' between the pair.

Once sex recognition has been achieved, the hen has to be put in the right mood to co-operate with the cock in mating—for rape is a practical impossibility in birds—and to accept him as a non-hostile partner for the duration of the breeding season. To achieve this, a system of signals that operates over a short range has been evolved, and these we call courtship displays. They may include elaborate and spectacular shows, like those of peacocks, put on as intimidating signals for the benefit of other cocks as well as for the hens, or simple display flights as shown by swifts. Owls, too, have their sexual displays, but not many of them have been described. As could be expected, colour and elaborate plumes play a relatively small role in the displays of those owls that have so far been studied.

Cock barn owls court their mates in weird postures, often in the dimly-lit surroundings of their nest sites. This ceremony is described by Eric Hosking and Cyril Newberry in their book entitled *Birds of the Night*. A pair of barn owls were sitting about 1ft(30.5cm) apart on a beam in an old farmyard barn where they were nesting . . .

> Both birds engaged in a twittering 'conversation' accompanied by beak snapping, after which the cock slowly stretched his head and neck upwards and puffed out his feathers. He looked grotesque with his head thrown well back and his beak open wide . . . and then began to sway his head from side to side, and presently to weave it in a somewhat circular motion. The hen started to sway in sympathy and to utter a snoring note as she did so and, at the same time, she edged up until she was close beside the cock. He then retracted his neck and lowered his head, and the two birds rubbed cheeks together. They followed this by a short bout of clicking their bills together, but the cock soon brought this to an end by seizing the hen by the neck feathers and swaying from side to side.

The authors comment that the hen seemed to like the rough treatment and purred intermittently during the course of it. Nevertheless, the pre-dominance of bill snapping and the seizure of the hen by the cock seems to reflect the knife-edge upon which courtship is based; that is, the conflict between treating a mate as a rival by attacking it, and responding to it as a sexual partner.

Cock tawny owls, in their courtship displays, apparently sway from side to side and vertically in front of their mates. While doing so, the wings are raised alternately and the plumage ruffled and then compressed; at one moment the actor looks like an 'animated ball' and then the whole appearance changes dramatically as the plumage is sleeked. Grunting noises are uttered throughout, and the conflict between approaching the hen and withdrawing from her is reflected in ambling movements along the branch towards and away from her. This spectacular display was recorded by Mr W. J. Churchill in the *History of the Birds of Suffolk*. Another charming account of the courtship of the great horned owl appears in *Life Histories of North American Birds of Prey*. Ruffling and wing raising again featured in the courtship, together with bowing movements. Bill snapping by the small cock indicated that there was a degree of conflict involved in the performance, which reached an interesting climax when a rabbit incautiously appeared on the scene. The cock rose, and in a clean, silent glide caught the prey, returned, and presented the prize to the hen. Together they devoured the rabbit, and afterwards both joined in the 'dance'.

The presentation of food is a common event in courtship displays; male Lycosid spiders, for instance, thrust either a real or empty food parcel into the jaws of their partner before attempting to mate. Evolutionarily speaking, this is a wise move because it prevents the female making a meal of her partner. Terns, finches, hawks and a host of other birds also include donation of food by the male in their pre-copulatory ceremonies, and there is evidence that courtship feeding may be necessary to supply the hen with enough nourishment to enable her to form a clutch of bulky eggs over a short period. In owls, too, this may be important, although doubtless the cock's act of presenting the larger fearsome hen with a tasty morsel arouses her interest in the food rather than in warding off her suitor. In this way, aggressive tendencies which would otherwise militate against co-operation between the pair are gradually broken down, and that is partly what courtship is about.

Fairly diurnal owls of open country, like the short-eared, have aerial displays involving wing clapping, and the snowy owl cock is reported to fly in circles high above the nest site. In this respect they are similar to other kinds of birds, which have adopted conspicuous advertising by flying, in places where this proves rather more practical than vocal or static displays; for example, the skylark, meadow pipit and whimbrel.

Once the hen owl's sex-drive has been aroused by mutual posturing, she invites the cock to mount her by uttering soft, repetitive 'begging' calls. The cock then knows he is safe, and that the otherwise dangerous act of jumping on to a larger and probably more powerful owl, equipped with a hooked beak and savage talons as sharp as any that birds have ever produced, can be accomplished without fear of reprisals. After they have copulated, the owls may preen themselves, and as time progresses owl partners will rest and roost, pressed against each other flank to flank, and will even preen each other's head plumage. The change in character is tremendous; mutual trust, and what can only be called friendliness, completely takes over from mutual suspicion.

The nest site is an area that is frequently displayed upon, because it is vital that both birds are fully decided upon its location. Cocks often perform nest advertising displays, and after the female has joined in, the position and details of the site are probably impressed on her mind; after all, this is the place where she will have to lay her eggs. The nest invitation display of the eagle owl looks very similar to the posturing of the snowy owl described on p55, involving a great deal of bill clappering and bowing.

By comparison with other birds, owls are not great homemakers. More often than not they rely upon the endeavours of other species, because they are basically hole or crevice nesters. Old woodpeckers' holes are frequently utilised; Tengmalm's owls in Europe often become squatters in the vacated burrows of great black woodpeckers, while across the Atlantic the tiny elf owl depends upon Gila woodpeckers and Mearns' gilded flickers to bore out nesting sites in the giant saguaro cactus. Indeed, owls and woodpeckers may even use the same cavity, the owls sleeping by day and moving out as the Gila woodpeckers come home to roost.

Elf owls are not totally dependent upon the giant saguaro forests, because these birds range widely over arid and semi-arid places, from grassy plains to forests up to an altitude of 7,000ft(2,133m). In fact, these owls have been on the decrease in the saguaro forests in Southern Arizona in the past few years, and one of the reasons may be the widespread spraying of cotton crops in that part of the world. The elf owl's diet consists chiefly of large insects, centipedes and moths, and the chicks are fed chiefly on arachnida (spiders, scorpions and their allies). Recently a pair was sent from the Arizona-Sonora Desert Museum to Washington Zoo where they bred in 1967. As reported in the *International Zoo Yearbook* for 1970, the tiny eggs were incubated, probably by both parents, for about three weeks, and when the three-day-old chick was discovered it measured only ½in(12mm). But after a month it had left the nest and was as large as its parents.

In mature forests there are always plenty of rotten trees, and if the woodpeckers have not provided for the owls, then cavities in stumps or decayed boles are ready for a take-over as owlet nurseries. Some species, such as the long-eared owl, prefer to nest outside and become tenants in bulky raptor or crows' nests. *Bubo* and *Strix* species

Long-eared owl, *Asio otus* (*Eric Hosking*)

regularly make their homes in the old nests of eagles, ravens, or even in squirrels' dreys.

Other owls have taken to nesting on the ground in adaptation to living in tree-bare habitats; examples of this are the short-eared and snowy owls. There are even records of the tawny and long-eared owls rearing chicks on terrestrial sites, which is perhaps curious for such traditionally arboreal species. The tawny and, doubtfully, the long-eared owls have also been noted nesting down rabbit burrows. Such adaptability has, of course, tremendous survival value for these owls, because they might be able to live and breed successfully in open areas should the right opportunities arise. On the other hand, in New Zealand, the laughing owl's very existence has been put in jeopardy through nesting on the ground, where it is particularly vulnerable to the depredations of introduced carnivores and rats. In the New World, the burrowing owl, as its name suggests, nests underground, usually in association with prairie-dog communities. Although they are able to dig their own tunnels, those deserted by ground squirrels, viscachas, wolves, foxes, skunks, and armadillos also tend to be requisitioned.

Nest sites are often used for many years. In the United States, a pair of barred owls rang the changes between five sites during their stay together of no less than twenty-six years. Owls have a long potential lifetime—the record is held by an eagle owl which lived for sixty-eight years— and should a pair manage to survive for an exceptionally long period, the chances are that they will return again and again to a favoured home.

As could be expected from birds which are basically ledge or cavity nesters, the owl's powers of building or repairing are either strictly limited or non-existent. The dusky and milky eagle owls of India and Africa respectively occasionally assemble platforms on which to nest, although they generally prefer to raise their young on ready-made sites. Among the *Strix* owls, the great gray is the only one which may build its own—described as a 'loose, artless platform of dry twigs through which the owlets could be seen from below'. Normally, they make their homes in the disused nests of raptors high in pine, birch or poplar trees. In such cases, the building operation only runs to the females adding a top dressing or new lining of pine needles or strips of bark. But once the nest is

Great grey owl adds some material to old nests

Horned owl using old raptor's nest

Elf owl nests in old woodpecker holes in Arizona cactus

Eagle owl nesting on rocky ledge

Burrowing owls nesting in disused prairie dog burrow

Snowy owls nest on open tundra

completed, there is no mistaking an incubating great gray owl. 'You would think a man was peering out of the nest'—as one Norwegian forester put it!

If, by comparison with other birds, owls appear to be indifferent homemakers, a purely anthropomorphic notion, then they excel themselves in the persistence and ferocity with which they will attack intruders. When tawny owls have eggs or chicks, they will make life uncomfortable, if not dangerous, for anyone who ventures too close to the nest by diving out of the darkness and striking the trespasser very hard. In suburban areas where these owls often breed, walkers out late at night are from time to time attacked, and they rarely suspect that they are passing too close to an owl's nest in some nearby tree. An owl's talons are razor-sharp and freely used, so every precaution should be taken when approaching owl breeding sites. Great gray owls will buffet intruders unmercifully, if not deliver ugly gashes to potential nest robbers.

Those which breed in open nests have a second line of defence no less spectacular than the attack—the defence display. Once seen, it is never forgotten. The owl faces the intruder, the body plumage is ruffled so that the bird apparently doubles in size, and the wings are rotated forwards and spread. The effect is rather that of a great

Long-eared owl - defensive attitude

White-faced Scops owl

Snowy owl

Spectacled owl

Elf owl

animated fan, made all the more frightening by the clappering bill and the big staring eyes. Even the downy owlets are able to scare off would-be assailants in this way because this dramatic behaviour develops at an early age and functions while the birds are still in the nest.

The eyes of owls pose a curious problem, because in most species they are so colourful and contrast markedly with the surrounding plumage. Eyes are usually an embarrassment to camouflaged animals, simply because they tend to be noticeable; they are often big, shiny, and circular, thereby drawing attention to themselves. Various tricks have been developed by highly cryptic animals in order to 'hide' their eyes from view; for example, dark eyes are hidden away in bands of black as in the case of the ringed plover, or else the lids can be partly shut, and this course of action is adopted by the otherwise beautifully camouflaged nightjars when sitting out the hours of

Flammulated owl

Barn owl

Saw-whet owl

Great grey owl

daylight. There seems little doubt however that owls, far from concealing their eyes, have positively made a feature of them. Some kinds have deep golden-brown irises, others are the palest lemon-yellow. Even a few of the black-eyed owls have white facial discs which set off their eyes wonderfully—as in the case of the barn owls—and in others, such as the short- and long-eared, the feathers around the face are so marked that the yellow eyes are enhanced. This phenomenon demands an explanation, and the answer might possibly be that their eyes are used to terrify their enemies.

It is a well-known fact that concentric ring patterns are used extensively in nature as intimidating signals. Certain butterflies and moths expose eye-like markings on their hind wings when they are worried by birds, and with quite dramatic results. Experiments on jays show that when they are suddenly confronted with a pair of big eye-spots, they lose all thoughts of hunger and are startled out of their wits, to say the least. There is even one species of moth (*Caligula*) which reveals its warning patterns in such a way that it closely resembles an owl; the results on predators must be singularly effective!

The eyes certainly add impact to the defence displays of owls. These are usually given on the nest sites, and are made even more effective by day because the pupils are small and the area of coloured iris is at its greatest. Even a roosting owl may be able to intimidate mobbing birds or squirrels by flashing its light-adapted eyes at them. Owlets have an in-built set of warning signals which they can present to an intruder sizing up the possibilities for an easy killing. It is even conceivable that iris constriction might accompany certain courtship or aggressive displays, as happens in many diurnal species of birds, and so the eyes would then have a short-distance intra-specific communication function. Should these theories prove correct, it would be of great interest to know why some owls in otherwise 'coloured' eye genera have black eyes, for example the flammulated owl, and vice versa, of course. All the *Strix* owls are dark-eyed except the great gray owl, which has small yellow eyes.

The ground-nesting snowy owl has to contend not only with aerial pirates like skuas and gulls, but also with formidable mammalian predators like Arctic foxes, which may be less easily deterred by static warning displays. In common with so many ducks, waders and sand grouse, these owls have distraction displays which work by luring the enemy away from the nest. Both owls may flop on to the ground belly first, and flap around in a clumsy way with wings outstretched. The behaviour resembles that of an injured bird and, lured by the prospects of an easy meal, the predator usually follows, thus moving away from the relatively vulnerable owlets, only to be taken aback when the apparently incapacitated parent owl suddenly leaps into the air and escapes. All this may be interspersed with aerial attacks as well.

Like those of most other hole-nesting birds, the eggs of owls are white. Presumably there is no need for camouflage in sites which are

Long-eared owls are particularly associated with conifer forests; they have a favourite roost-tree, marked on the ground by a circle of droppings and pellets (*Hans Reinhard/Bruce Coleman Ltd*)

Snowy owls are birds of the Arctic tundra (*Steven Kaufman/Bruce Coleman Ltd*)

basically well hidden. Indeed, pale shells may even be an advantage inside the dark recesses of trees or caves where many owls make their home, because they would be more easily detected by the sensitive eyes of the parents. Even those species which habitually nest in fairly exposed sites lay white eggs, but they are protected by the camouflage of the incubating owl. A similar situation prevails in many other kinds of birds; pheasants, partridges, ducks, and geese, all have unmarked eggs, but the hen birds are always dispersed, and therefore difficult to find. They match their surroundings to a high degree, and sit tight.

Species with camouflaged eggs often leave the nest if they are disturbed, and the eggs have temporarily to look after themselves; as for example those of terns, gulls and waders. The eggs of owls also tend to be more spherical than most; this may also be an adaptation to hole-nesting. Exaggerated pyriform eggs are laid by species which nest in exposed, precarious positions, where the clutch could be easily smashed by rolling. Guillemots, which jostle together on breeding ledges, produce eggs which spin rather than roll, and so their very survival depends as much on their pear-shaped eggs as on their own ability to catch fish or copulate. Since many owls nest at the bottom of shafts or deep crevices, there is no need to have eggs of special construction, because by the very nature of the sites the

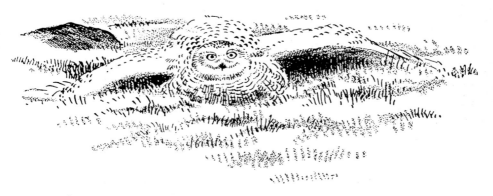

Snowy owl in distraction display - based on photographs by K. Richmond

clutch will always be kept together. It is interesting that the great gray owl, nesting in open sites, has eggs which are more oval shaped than its hole-nesting cousins—the Ural and tawny. Of course, pear-shaped eggs will always fit neatly together in the nest and make for easier incubation, but this factor seems to be unimportant to owls.

The number of eggs in each clutch varies tremendously in the owl family. Many eagle owls lay single-egg clutches, whereas others, like the burrowing owl, may produce nearly a dozen. Tropical owls on the whole lay smaller clutches than species of more northerly latitudes; the average clutch in equatorial Africa is 2.5, as opposed to 4.6 in mid-Europe.

The timing of the breeding season and the family size both have great survival value for owls, and have been determined by evolutionary processes of natural selection. Eggs are laid so that the period of chick development coincides with the time when there is a maximum of food. In this way, the greatest number of chicks that a pair of owls can support are reared. Similarly, there is evidence that the average clutch size represents the greatest number of chicks that a pair could possibly rear, for monogamy is usually the rule in owls, although there are several records of snowy owl cocks turning to bigamy. The odd vast clutch belonging to short-eared owls leads one to suspect that this species also occasionally indulges in polygamy; one found in Finland in 1911 had no less than 16 eggs. Admittedly, this occurred during a vole plague when hens tended to lay more eggs than usual. However, if there are too many owlets the parents would be unable to cope and the chances are that food would be wasted on young which would probably starve; the survival of the whole brood might even be jeopardised. On the other hand, artificially smaller broods would not necessarily be in the species' own interests; although the owlets would wax on a superabundant food supply, rather like spoilt children, recruitment into the population might not make good the natural mortality of the adults. In other words, not enough owlets would be produced to keep the population up. For each species a balance has to be struck, depending upon what kind of food is taken by the parents, how long they tend to live, and so on.

On top of this, however, there are further refinements. Some owls are automatically able to adjust their family sizes according to how

Short-eared owl, *Asio flammeu (Arthur Gilpin)*

much food there is around. This is clearly a modification built into
the reproductive machinery of owls, and indeed of other birds also,
which have to face a widely varying food supply. At one extreme,
breeding may be given up altogether in years when rodent food is
scarce, and in peak years clutches may be extraordinarily high,
numbering a dozen or more eggs in the case of the short-eared owls.
Obviously, the ease with which prey can be caught at the time of
egg-laying somehow determines just how many eggs will be laid, or
not as the case may be. There is yet a further sophistication, which
can be likened to a rough kind of birth control, whereby the
production of young is tuned to the available resources of the habitat.

Incubation starts as soon as the hen starts laying, and this can be
at intervals of two days or so. There is a record of a great gray owl
laying at twelve-day intervals! Since the period of development
inside the egg is constant, the hatching of the owlets will be
staggered, or asynchronous. By the time the last owlet chick chips
its way out into the world, the first one could be as much as two
weeks old, with more than a head start over its younger sibling.
Since parent owls, and owlets too for that matter, have no feelings
of fair play, the largest and strongest chicks in the nest will dominate
the food. Therefore, when rodents and insects are plentiful, the
demands of the first-hatched owlets will be satisfied, and only when
their screams for pieces of meat die down and they are in a contented
and unaggressive state, will the needs of the smaller ones be met.

Large broods may, therefore, be raised when conditions are
favourable, but when the hunting is indifferent the smaller members
of the family may quickly succumb to starvation. When hungry
enough it is not beyond the older members of the brood to fill their
stomachs on their younger brothers and sisters. Incontrovertible
evidence for such apparently revolting acts of cannibalism came from
a video camera recording the domestic life of a family of tawny
owls nesting in a barn in Holland—this was part of a study being
carried out by Dr Joop von Veen of the University of Wageningen.
When played back, the tapes revealed scenes of the adults returning
to the nestlings with mice, rats, and voles; occasionally, one of the
parents entered the dim spotlight drenching wet with a frog impaled
on its talons! Despite the succession of food items, the smallest chick
lost ground and eventually succumbed to starvation. After it had

expired, the hen gently nudged the tiny, fluffy corpse a few times as though to make sure that it was beyond hope, then suddenly clenched it in her claws and tore it apart. She fed the pieces to her remaining ever-hungry offspring. The final ghoulish scene captured by Dr Von Veen's camera was of one of the owlets choking on the head of its younger deceased sibling!

Thus staggered hatching is rather like a natural insurance policy. It is both simple and effective; after all, if a sudden famine should strike, one or two healthy owlets are better than half-a-dozen starving ones whose chances of fledging are poor. Not all owls show staggered hatching. The eggs of the pigmy owl, for example, tend to hatch synchronously, and this means that incubation commences with the laying of the last egg.

In most owls, it is the hen which takes on the long vigil of incubating the eggs, and she does so with such dedication that she only rarely leaves her precious charge in order to defecate. Here possibly is the clue as to why female owls are so much bulkier than their mates. It was once thought that the disparity in size enabled the sexes to hunt different prey, thereby not competing too seriously with each other. This explanation gains some credence from the nature of the victims brought back to the nest by parent pigmy owls. At first, when the cock alone is providing all the sustenance for both his mate and her brood, the menu consists of relatively small birds. But as the young owls' demand grows, the larger hen joins in the hunting forays, and suddenly medium-sized species like great spotted woodpeckers and song thrushes are brought back to the nest—and these are beyond the capturing ability of the cock. So why should hen owls always be the heftier of the sexes?

It is thought that a big body should be of value to the hen in her role as the sole incubator. Although her mate plies her with food, there is evidence—especially in the cool northern forests—that hen owls lose weight and perhaps condition during their lengthy sojourn on their eggs. Outside, the temperature may slump to $20°$ C below zero, but the metabolic fires within her body must maintain the

(*overleaf*) Long-eared owls usually take over the old tree nest of another species; the chicks remain in it for about three-and-a-half weeks (*R.T. Mills/ Aquila Photographics*)

clutch virtually at blood heat. While the cock Tengmalm's owl has no difficulty keeping up his weight, his mate drops from 6½ to 5¼oz (189 to 148g) as she burns her fat reserves to generate the heat that sustains the lives stirring inside the eggs. In this situation, the hen's enhanced mass has survival value because it generates much needed calories. The males' best interests are served by being light and manoeuvrable, all the better to intercept nimble-footed rodents.

Incubation takes three to five weeks. When the chicks hatch both parents bring home the bounties of their hunting. At first the food is processed; the heads of birds and rodents are usually ripped off and devoured by the adults before the prey is given to the owlets. Later on the victims' skulls may simply be crushed. Observations at barn owl nests show that at first the chicks were fed rather small mammals, such as field voles, mice and shrews, whereas after they were three weeks old rats started to appear on the menu. That the parents have to work hard to catch enough food for themselves and their family can be taken for granted. While keeping watch over and photographing a barn owl's nest, Eric Hosking recorded no less than ninety-one short-tailed field voles, twenty-one rats, eight common shrews, two long-tailed mice, one mole, and a pigmy shrew brought in for the four chicks. The total catch must have been much greater.

At seven weeks, young barn owls are as large as their parents. Although their bodies are still clad in down, the wing feathers and juvenile plumage are developing fast and, not long after, the owlets take their first flight. The fledgling period is probably shorter for long-eared owls which tend to nest in more vulnerable exposed sites; the sooner the young can fly, the better, and they leave the nest well before they are four weeks old.

Once outside the nest, the problems are not over for either owlets or their parents. Survival is not just a matter of flying, because the fledglings must first of all learn to hunt efficiently and this takes time. In tawny owls at least, the parents must supply their offspring with voles and mice well into the autumn, and it is not until then that the juveniles make their own way in the world. Months of trial and error will have made some of them reasonably skilful in the art of being killers, but the real test will come when they have to fight for, or take over, a vacant territory of their own, and thereafter support themselves by their own endeavours. Not many owlets will

Young barn owls showing difference in age between the first and last to be hatched

reach this stage. If food is scarce, the youngsters will be the first to suffer, and late in the summer exhausted and wasted fledglings are by no means a rare occurrence.

Ringing studies show how heavily the dice are loaded against a new generation of owls. At Wytham, in Oxford, tawny owls only managed to rear on average between 0.1 to 1.3 chicks per pair in years when they attempted to breed. Elsewhere on the continent of Europe, where the owls were not nesting as densely as in Wytham, up to 3.5 young per pair each year has been recorded. In Switzerland, the annual mortality of ringed tawny owl chicks was 47 per cent for the first year of life, reducing to 45 per cent during the second year, and levelling off to 24 per cent in subsequent years. If the mortality seems high, then the figures for Sweden are even higher. Sixty-seven out of every hundred ringed tawny owl fledglings die in their first year, and of every hundred that survive each year, forty-three will be lost in each subsequent year. Clearly life is a tenuous commodity to young owls, and the odds are very great that each owlet will be picked up dead either in June as a result of starvation through lack of parental feeding, or in the following March when they have been weakened by the hard winter. If it manages to cope with both these crises, then the outlook for the tawny owl at least looks brighter, and once it reaches adulthood then each year there is a three-in-four chance of it living a further year.

Of course, these statistics do not hold good for the taiga and tundra species, where the food supply fluctuates so wildly and widely that in some years nearly all the offspring will manage to survive. However, as will be gathered from reading Chapter 3, the crash must be only a year or two away, and then owls and a host of other raptors will drop out of the sky in thousands, if not millions.

Owls are, on the whole, stay-at-home birds, and although the year's crop of owlets will have to seek their fortunes other than in their parents' territories, they will try and fit into neighbouring territories left vacant, perhaps by the death of an adult; accordingly, most travel no more than 6½miles(10km) from their parents' nest. Since most territories will be occupied, the majority will be doomed to early deaths. Occasionally, young owls move further afield; there is a record of a tawny owl chick ringed on 7 May 1952 at Budle, Northumberland, being recovered seventy miles away at Wamphray in Dumfriesshire on 4 November of the same year. For a British-bred bird, this owl was especially hard-travelling! However, there is a quite exceptional record of a tawny owl ringed in Finland being found in southern Russia 1,250miles(1,960km) away.

Nevertheless, the young of some owls do face long journeys in the autumn of their first year. The insectivorous scops owl is migratory, breeding in southern Europe and wintering in North Africa, where its food is more abundant at that time of the year. The oriental hawk owls, too, in the northern parts of their range, migrate to the Celebes, Philippines, and Malaysia in the winter. Long-eared owls are also migratory, in Europe making journeys of up to 1,300miles(2,000km) on a broad front. There is even a well-defined passage at high Swiss mountain passes such as the Col de Bretolet. In the British Isles, the numbers of the residents are swollen by continental immigrants. Owls ringed in Sweden, Holland and Heligoland have all been recovered in the United Kingdom. Snowy, hawk, Tengmalm's, and great gray owls may move to winter quarters, although these taiga and tundra owls, together with the short-eareds, are, more in the nature of nomadic than regular migrants.

As the days draw in, the home life of the owls comes to an end. Families will split up, and though pairs may continue to inhabit the same territories, the prevailing mood will change because independ-

Young tawny owls venture out of the nesthole and wander about just before
they can fly (*G.F. Date/Aquila Photographics*)

ence will replace the co-operation of the breeding season. Tolerance
for the owlets which have been so carefully, and perhaps painstak-
ingly, reared will be overtaken by rank hostility. The lean months
of winter, whether in the tropics or high Arctic, are coming and
very owl must fend for itself.

3 *Numbers of Owls*

Owls are killers by nature. They take all manner of prey, from insects, earthworms, fish and amphibians to quite large birds and mammals. Whatever the prey, owls are perceptive and swift in the hunt, and deadly in the strike. As part of nature's array of butchers, it would seem that, with the world teeming with potential food, they have life all their way but this is far from the truth. The fact that the hooting of owls does not fill the night, as the twittering of song birds pervades the day, suggests that something must be holding the numbers of these nocturnal predators in check. What then limits the size of their populations, and why do certain kinds seem to be far more numerous some years than in others?

Inevitably, predators are less numerous than the animals upon which they feed. They must be, or else they would eat themselves out of business. Vast populations of herbivorous mammals, like the gnu, provide a living for a pride of lions; similarly, a pair of barn owls probably need at least seventy to eighty acres of hunting territory to find enough rodents over the year to satisfy their food requirements without exterminating the prey species. Small song birds, on the other hand, need only a fraction of an acre. So the density of birds like song thrushes or chaffinches will always be higher than that of owls. This is called the pyramid of numbers, and demonstrates the fact that animals further up the food chain tend to be less numerous than those at the bottom. Thus insects are far more common than the shrews which feed upon them, which in turn are more abundant than the owls which snatch them from the leaf litter. This concept of the food chain and the pyramid of numbers gives us a clue to the checks that are maintained on owl populations.

The most likely factor limiting the populations of owls is their food supply. Owls are hunters, and the animals upon which they depend do not sit around waiting to be caught. They are elusive and, in the depth of winter, can be particularly thin on the ground. At this time of the year the life of the hunter is not easy, and those that fail to make consistent catches starve.

Some studies have been made on how the number and concentration of food animals influences owl populations, and such investigations have been made all the easier because these birds produce an involuntary record of their past feasts. Owls tend to bolt their food whole. Luckily for the inquisitive naturalist, the gastric juices of owls are relatively less acid than diurnal birds of prey (pH about 2.35) and so the bones and teeth of their victims tend to be preserved. After the nourishing soft parts have been dissolved, the indigestible fur, bones, teeth, fragments of insect exoskeletons, and even the minute chitinous bristles from the body walls of earthworms, are regurgitated as tightly packed pellets rather than voided as faeces. There seems to be a need to produce casts, which means that a certain amount of roughage must be taken in, and this is normally supplied with the natural food. There is, however, an account of a tame little owl which presumably failed to eat enough roughage, and regurgitated a pellet of hard insect remains neatly packaged with elastic bands, which it had found in its temporary lodging place.

The size, shape, and even the colouring of the pellets is sometimes diagnostic of the species that produced them, although their proper-

Barn owl

Tawny owl

Long-eared owl

OWL PELLETS

Little owl

beetle remains
rodent remains

Tengmalm's owl

Short-eared owl

Pellets may be dissected
by soaking in warm water
and then separated on
blotting paper using
tweezers and needles.
A good lens is useful
in identifying the remains
of animals and insects.

Analysis of pellets provides
excellent clues to the food
being taken.
Some of the more usual
and obvious items are shown
here (not to scale), skulls and
jaws of small birds and mammals,
fur and feathers and the hard
wing cases of beetles.

ties will depend to some extent upon the owl's diet at the time. Large owls cough up large pellets; those of the barn owl are often characteristically blackish and have a varnished look about them. Short-eared owls produce a pellet for every 1-3oz(30-90g) of food taken, although barn owls will eject several small ones if the hunting is poor. On average, two pellets are formed each day and these are often deposited at daytime roosts, or even nest-sites. Barn owls tend to remain faithful to their hideouts year in and year out, so that large numbers of pellets may accumulate in one place. Tawny owls, on the other hand, tend to change their roosting sites quite often, and so the indigestible remains of their meals will accordingly be dispersed.

But are the results of pellet analysis a reliable guide to the food intake of the owls? Experiments conducted with owls suggest that if a number of rodents are fed to these birds, a corresponding number of skulls, or matching sets of jaws, can be recovered from the subsequently ejected pellets. Although sophisticated scientific techniques can be used to assess the contents of intact pellets, such as X-ray photography, the best way to discover what they contain is either to soften the dry casts of fur and bone in water, or to tease them apart directly. Their contents can be examined under a microscope if necessary, and the composition of the owl's diet discovered. Small mammals can easily be identified by the shape and pattern of enamel and softer dentine of their teeth; birds from their skulls and beaks. Some owls, like the tawny, may make the business of pellet analysis more difficult because they do not always bolt their food whole. The skulls of their victims may be crushed before they are swallowed and, in any case, very fragile crania, or brain cases, may not stand up to the acid stomach juices of the owls. Birds are sometimes inconveniently decapitated, although their pelvic girdles may provide the necessary clues to enable the species to be identified.

Owl pellets are very valuable objects both to the nature detective and to the professional field ecologist who are involved in fathoming out the relationship between these predators and their prey. Before turning to the latter subject, it might be of interest to look at some of the discoveries which have been made by people studying pellets. Giant barn owls that used to live in the Caribbean have left us the remains of their meals as fossilised pellets, and this is one of the few cases where we know for certain the food of long since dead animals.

It was the evidence from pellets which was used to incriminate the Cape barn owl as the killer of protected birds on Cousin Island in the Indian Ocean. This big owl was introduced into the Seychelles over ten years ago to combat the rat menace in the coconut plantations, but the local birds proved more easily caught than the rodents. This was the indisputable story yielded by the pellets, studied by members of a Bristol University expedition who found that, far from containing the bony remains of rodents, the pellets were more often than not stuffed with the skulls and feathers of young terns and noddies. The owls are now themselves hunted, and are shown no mercy, particularly on Cousin Island, which was bought for £15,500 by the International Council for Bird Protection, and is now managed as a nature reserve because of its unique and relatively unspoilt bird colonies. Apart from being an interesting piece of detective work, the story also shows the dangers of introducing foreign species into new surroundings. Doubtless Cape barn owls exist chiefly on small mammals in their own habitat, but when faced with an enormous supply of easy food in the form of defenceless chicks, the most ardent rodent killer is likely to turn its talons to an easier living, with disastrous results on the established animal community. A happier story is that, also by means of pellet analysis, little owls were exonerated as game and poultry thieves in the British Isles–the full tale of this investigation is told in Chapter 4.

Some owls are extremely good samplers of the small mammal populations in their hunting territories; indeed, in the first instance, naturalists can do no better than consult the indigestible fragments left by wise old owls before attempting to survey the mammal fauna of most habitats by other means. For example, the remains of wood mice in the pellets of tawny owls gave away the presence of these elusive rodents, hitherto unsuspected, in Central London. One of the few records of harvest mice in North Wales turned up incarcerated in the pellets of a local owl. In America, red-backed pine mice were discovered in central Connecticut because skulls of this species turned up in the pellets of barn owls roosting in the college belfry in Middletown. A search of suitable habitats revealed a small colony nearby, where the owls were obviously hunting.

Little owl, *Athene noctua*, with field mouse (*Eric Hosking*)

Long-term studies of owl pellets can also be used to monitor changes that may be taking place in the small mammal community of the owl's hunting area. Patrick Morris, a British mammalogist, has always realised the value of these birds in his studies, and he has reported the changes in diet forced on a barn owl by an alteration in vegetation. In 1961, the territory under survey was basically overgrown, wet meadows of long grass, thistles and nettles. Short-tailed voles, a mammal characteristic of tussocky grass, made up nearly 60 per cent by weight of an owl's diet. By 1964, the introduction of grazing horses had turned this rough piece of wilderness into open expanses of turf, and the alteration in the resident mammal population was reflected in the changed composition of the pellets of the owl. Short-tailed voles dropped by nearly one half, to 32 per cent, and their bones were replaced by those of wider-ranging mammals like rats (10 per cent), wood mice (23.5 per cent), and bank voles (20 per cent), which were now able to wander over the open fields quartered by the owl. A thorough trapping campaign could not have been more effective in recording the impact of grazing on the small mammal community.

Sometimes pellets, incidentally, yield very interesting and not easily obtainable information about the behaviour of mammals. For example, moles regularly turn up in the menu of tawny and barn owls. Indeed, in one owl study these 'velvet diggers' accounted for nearly one half by weight of the food intake of tawny owls between May and October. Clearly, these birds do not go hunting down the underground tunnels of moles, and so the obvious conclusion to draw is that moles visit the surface or scrape around beneath the moss or leaf litter rather more often than we might otherwise have suspected.

By dissecting a large number of pellets collected from a single roost over the course of a year or two, the menu of its residents, one or a pair, can be drawn up in terms of so many rats, field voles, chaffinches and so on. Interesting through this information is, it is not particularly meaningful, because it is useful to know just how much each species contributed to the total food intake of the owls. These birds are to some extent opportunists and the medium and large species in Europe will take mammals such as minute pigmy shrews on the one hand, to comparatively hefty brown rats or rabbits on the other. Clearly, a diet sheet consisting entirely of small insectivores and comparatively large rodents or lagomorphs in almost equal proportions by number would tend to mask the fact that the pigmy shrews contributed very little to the bulk of the diet. An owl like a tawny or barn would have to catch large numbers of small prey species and therefore would have to expend a great deal of energy if it were to live on pigmy or even common shrews alone; after all, the nutritional requirements of an owl remain the same whether it exists on small or large prey. Of course, this rather depends on how easy the prey is to catch and how available it is at the time. All things being equal, the larger species find it more economical to tackle larger prey species, and it could be predicted that this would be reflected in the results of pellet analyses.

In order to assess the relative nutritional value of each prey species in an owl's diet, 'conversion factors' are applied by field workers taking a ¾oz(20g) rodent as a standard, and the total eight of each prey species is then expressed in either 'prey units', or as a straight percentage. Short-tailed and bank voles, house and wood mice weigh approximately 20g and have a conversion factor of one, whereas the pigmy and common shrews are much lighter, and their conversion factors are 0.2 and 0.5 respectively; that is to say one pigmy shrew is equivalent to one-fifth of a 20g mammal, and the heavier bank vole is about equal to half a 'standard rodent'. Twenty-five pigmy shrews or five bank voles are equivalent in weight to one mole or brown rat; these bulky mammals have conversion factors of five; that is, they are equivalent to five 20g animals. To see how all this works out in practice, here are the results of an analysis of long-eared owl pellets taken from a roost in Ireland.

Altogether the remains of 955 wood mice, seventy-nine house mice, fifty-six brown rats, ten pigmy shrews, and fifty-seven birds were found. Although the number of brown rats seems to be insignificant in this survey (ie, fifty-six out of a total of 1,157 animals, or about 5 per cent), after these figures are converted the percentage by weight of the individual prey species turns out to be: wood mice 70 per cent, brown rats 20 per cent, house mice 6 per cent, and birds 4 per cent.

Let us see how the picture of predator and prey populations works in practice, because although many people hold the view that nature

'balances' itself out, with the implication that animal populations are static, this is a far cry from the truth.

One of the most detailed pieces of research into the relationship between owls and the animals upon which they feed was carried out in Wytham Wood, near Oxford, in England, by Dr H. N. Southern. His subject was the tawny owl, a species that is widespread in open, broad-leaved woodlands and parklands throughout Europe and parts of East Asia. Up to thirty pairs nested in the 1,000-acre study area. Their diet was monitored by direct observation of the prey as it was brought back to specially constructed nest-boxes, which were floodlit with red light, and also through analysis of pellets.

In Wytham, the almost entirely nocturnal wood mouse (*Apodemus sylvaticus*), and the 'twenty-four hour' bank vole (*Clethrionomys glareolus*), comprised 60 per cent or so of the tawny owl's diet. Short-tailed voles (*Microtus agrestis*), common shrew (*Sorex araneus*), young rabbits (*Oryctolagus cuniculus*), and moles (*Talpa europaea*) made up the rest of the vertebrate items. Of the insects, beetles were by far the most common, including cockchafers, dor beetles (*Geotrupes* species), and burying beetles (*Necrophorus* species). The tawny owl, then, is by no means a food specialist in Wytham Wood, although in other areas it may have less choice. (See illustration overleaf.)

Suburban and city owls have quite a different economy, and in Central London, for instance, they prey heavily upon birds, particularly house sparrows, which are snatched from their roosts. These also account for 31 per cent of prey taken by tawny owls living in Holland Park, West London, with thrushes, blackbirds, and starlings accounting for another 37 per cent, and pigeons and jays a further 25 per cent. The remaining 7 per cent was composed of small mammals (see p 133). In their woodland homes, hunting tawny owls sit close to the ground, watch, and pounce, and most of their food is taken from the woodland floor, but indirectly they are deriving energy from all levels of the forest and the surrounding pastures. Wood mice and bank voles, both woodland species, can be regarded as packets of protein converted from beechmast, acorns, and other scrub fruits and seeds. Birds can also be regarded in a similar way. Earthworms derive whatever goodness is left from leaves when these

Tengmalm's owl with prey (*Kevin Carlson/Aquila Photographics*)

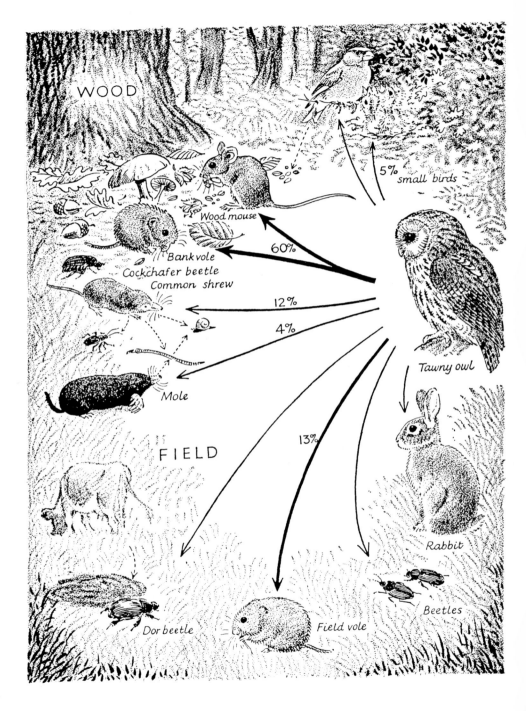

WOOD

5% small birds

Wood mouse

60%

Bank vole
Cockchafer beetle
Common shrew

12%

4%

Mole

Tawny owl

FIELD

13%

Rabbit

Dor beetle

Field vole

Beetles

reach the forest floor, and moles are, in economic terms, converted earthworms and other soil invertebrates. The food chain of the owls can be traced even to the productive grasses and clovers of the pasture, too, as shown by the appearance of open grassland species like short-tailed voles in their diet sheets.

Populations of prey species rarely stay constant from month to month, or from one year to another, and these variations can have a marked effect upon their predators. In Wytham, the density of the tawny owl's chief rodent prey species fluctuated from five to fifty individuals per acre. This was dependent upon the yields of beech-mast and other fruits; thus each pair of owls had up to 1,500 small rodents on their 30-acre hunting plots. Natural catastrophies like the outbreak of myxomatosis in 1954, which reduced the rabbit population drastically, made foxes and stoats turn to mice and voles for their living and this brought them more than usually into direct competition with tawny owls, which in turn had less of the rodent productivity 'cake'. Forestry practice, too, can make a great deal of difference to making the prey more or less abundant, or more or less available to the owls; for example, the clearance of undergrowth to some extent helps tawny owls to locate scuttling rodents and shrews.

How did the tawny owls adjust to a widely varying supply of food? Dr Southern found that although the number of breeding pairs remained the same in both good and bad rodent years, their breeding success varied greatly. For example, in 1958 both wood mice and bank voles were extremely scarce and not one of the thirty pairs of owls even attempted to nest. In a more normal year, at least three out of four pairs could be expected to lay eggs. In fact, the whole success of breeding is geared to the density of rodent prey, and therefore directly to the availability of food. In good mouse years, the clutches averaged three eggs or so, whereas in the poor rodent years of 1951 and 1955, fewer eggs were produced. In these years only a quarter of the eggs hatched, and this stems from the fact that the hens take charge of incubating them, relying upon the male to feed her with unremitting energy. If food is scarce, then the males, with less of a sense of chivalry and devotion than is expected of human husbands, give their own appetites priority and cause their mates, through hunger, to forsake the eggs. Needless to say, in years of comparative famine, very few young are reared (an average of

0.3 per pair as opposed to 0.9 per pair in good years).

Nearly a quarter of a century ago in the United States, John and Frank Craighead made a thorough study of the relationship between predatory birds and their prey. Each spent more than 800 days in the field systematically collecting data, chiefly in thirty-six square miles of Superior township, Michigan, and in a further square mile of the neighbouring Ann Arbor township. The area is a chequerboard of small woodlands, copses and cultivated land devoted to raising forage crops. So far as the owls were concerned, long-eared and short-eared wintered there; horned and screech owls were residents. Over the thirty-six square miles, there were only eleven great horned owls, each with a winter territory about half a mile in radius, based upon woodland areas. This is, in fact, a very low density for this large American eared owl, because in one area of California a total of seventeen horned owls were counted in 2,000 acres (that is, one per 188 acres). In Superior township, as elsewhere, this species proved to be a very versatile predator and hunted anything that was abundant; overall, however, the economy of these and other raptors was geared to meadow and white-footed mice.

The populations of these two rodent species were reckoned to be in the region of 303,000 and 33,000 respectively in 1941–2, whereas in 1947–8 the prey density was much less; about 75,000 meadow mice and 27,000 white-footed mice were present. Clearly, food was more abundant in 1941–2 than six years later, and not surprisingly the density of birds of prey was much higher when food was more readily available. Although the number of horned owls stayed the same during both periods, seven long-eared owls and up to thirty-one short-eared owls overwintered in 1941, when the latter was the commonest resident species. During the second period, when mice were less common, no long-eared owls were recorded and only four short-eared owls put in an appearance in the area in the late winter. Therefore the number of these nomadic and migratory species that settled in the area reflected the density of mouse prey.

Owls could not, of course, be considered in complete isolation, because they had to compete with other raptors for the food supply. During the fall and winter red-tailed, red-shouldered, and rough-legged hawks (buzzards) all consumed a high proportion of meadow mice; similarly, marsh hawks (hen harriers) existed almost entirely

on these rodents. Like the short-eared and long-eared owl populations, the number of these birds of prey also varied according to the
supply of their chief winter food. The owl and raptor winter density
in 1941–2 was just over four birds per square mile, and during the
same period in 1947–8 this was cut by one half to just over two per
square mile.

It can clearly be seen, then, that the density of owls in the study
area was proportional to the availability of food, and that migrant
species like the short-eared owl tend to settle wherever opportunities
for good hunting exist. That predators like short-eared owls are
quite prepared to concentrate was shown well when brown lemmings
(*Lemmus trimucronatus*) were particularly abundant in Alaska during
1953; these birds then capitalised upon this rich supply of food, and
wherever the lemmings swarmed the owls settled in concentrations
of up to seven pairs per square mile (one pair for nearly 100 acres).

In the Old World, too, these owls are inveterate wanderers, with
a high continental breeding range, restricted to open, treeless country
and moorlands. In years when their prey species are especially
numerous, the owls are able to settle in unusually large numbers to
breed and their success in rearing young is assured. Between the
years 1874 and 1876 there was a plague of short-tailed voles of
almost unprecedented proportions on the upland pastures of Eskdale,
in Dumfriesshire. The grass appeared to be seething with voles, and,
needless to say, the number of predatory owls quartering the ground
was higher than usual. In all, there were reckoned to be about 500
pairs of short-eared owls in the area and they bred without intermis-
sion from February to September, and clutches of ten to twelve
were reported to be not unusual. In their breeding at least, this
species is similar to the tawny owl; when food is plentiful the
clutches are high. The plague died out in 1877, and the owls left for
better pastures; those that remained starved. Years of plenty were
followed by famine.

Rodent population cycles, and the fluctuating fortunes of the birds
and mammals which depend upon them, are nowhere seen better
than in the relatively uniform environments girdling the northern
polar region—the *taiga* and *tundra*. The taiga is virtually a sea of
conifers that stretches across Eurasia and North America. To the
north, it merges into the tundra, and to the south it grades into

deciduous woodlands. Spruces, larches, and pines are the predominant trees of the taiga in Eurasia, with a scattering of birch, aspen and alder. The animals that populate this habitat tend to fluctuate rhythmically, and in peak years break out or move *en masse* from their normal home ranges. Pigmy, Lapland, Tengmalm's (or boreal) and hawk owls are the typical taiga species, and the last three at least show the characteristic oscillation between low and high density populations and irruptions. These cycles have quite a regular periodicity of around four years or so, and they can be traced back to the rhythmic production of seeds of the major tree species; this phenomenon naturally has repercussions on the animals whose economy is geared to them.

The Norway spruce (*Picea abies*) produces high yields of cones every third or fourth year in southern Sweden, and cone-rich years are followed by a year in which hardly any seeds at all are made. Crossbills, redpolls and siskins all feed their young with spruce seeds, and in good cone years the breeding success of these species is high. In years following a good and prolific breeding season, when the cone supply is exhausted, vast numbers of these birds fly far and wide, even to the shores of the Mediterranean, in search of sufficient food. Similarly, great spotted wood-peckers, which feed on spruce and Scots pine seeds, will also be fecund when the crop is good, but in low yield years these irrupt from the taiga.

Red squirrels, which are preyed upon by pine martens, goshawks and buzzards, also follow the rhythm of the spruce fructification. These rodents feed both upon the flower buds and the seeds which mature a year later, and so they are able to experience two consecutive winters of abundant food. In a good seed year the breeding is successful and there is a population explosion of red squirrels. However, when their food supply is suddenly and drastically reduced after a peak cone year they die in large numbers. In 1943, when there was a large-scale irruption of spruce-feeding birds from Scandinavia, the red squirrels were reduced to about 1/450 of their former abundance in a few months. Birds at least have the advantage over mammals through their increased mobility, because they can fly hundreds if not thousands of miles looking for better supplies of food.

Great horned owl, *Bubo virginiamus*, with grey squirrel (*Leonard Lee Rue III*)

Once the spruce seeds reach the ground they constitute an important source of nourishment for micro-rodents like wood lemmings (*Myopus schisticolor*) and various mice and voles. In peak seed-production years these mammals increase in number because the food supply supports a higher than usual population, and, with their very high fecundity, they may reach 'plague' proportions in a relatively short time. These, in turn, are preyed upon by various kinds of raptors and owls which raise large numbers of chicks when their food is plentiful. In 1943, when rodents were abundant in southern Sweden, hawk, short-eared and Tengmalm's owls were especially numerous and had presumably settled and bred well in the areas swarming with these small mammals. A food chain is therefore established; starting with the rhythmic flowering and fruiting of trees, to ground-living rodents, to predatory owls, which ultimately depend upon the productivity of plants for their survival.

All good things must come to an end and when the seed supplies are exhausted and the trees hardly fruit at all in the season following peak ones, then the rodent population crashes and the majority of the animals which prey upon them are left to starve, or to wander off in search of new hunting grounds. At these times birds of the taiga turn up in areas outside their 'normal' home ranges. For example, hawk owls regularly irrupt into Norway in 'fair numbers' and are recorded in districts where they are otherwise practically unknown. The rhythm of the cycles is quite noticeable: 1876, '80, '81, '87, '90, '96, '99, 1901, '03, '04, '05, '06, '12, '20, '27, '30, '31, '34, '48, '49, '50. At the time of these irruptions it will usually be found that voles and lemmings had been abundant earlier in the year, either in neighbouring areas or in Finland or Sweden. Rich sources of food therefore depress the mobility of these and other taiga-inhabiting birds, but when stocks run low whole populations start moving. Fructification rhythms are found not only in the spruce but also in other species, and this may be an adaptation to secure the maximum survival rate of the fruit over a period of years.

In the northerly coniferous forests of North America there is a ten-year population cycle of the varying hare (*Lepus americanus*) and, not unexpectedly, the numbers of the animals that prey upon it, such as the lynx and horned owl, follow suit. The renowned Hudson Bay Fur Trapping Company has been of enormous help to people studying animal populations in North America because their returns of trapped mammals give a good indication of their abundance from year to year. Peak years for the varying hare in Ontario were recorded in 1857, '65, '76, '87, '96, 1905, '14, '24, '34, and '43. Lynx were correspondingly abundant in these years, whereas Toronto was invaded by horned owls in 1888, '97, 1906, '16, '27, and '36; that is, often in years following the peaks of their chief source of food. These owls were presumably on the move from the food-scarce areas and on the look-out for fresh hunting grounds. In Labrador, horned owls live on voles which have four-year cycles, and here the owls take up the population rhythm of their prey species. Although most of the horned owls were doomed to a slow death by starvation, some presumably stumbled on good supplies of food because elsewhere the varying hare may have been abundant; indeed this North American rabbit 'peaked' somewhere in Canada every year between 1939 and 1946. The advantage to the species of wandering are therefore obvious; although many will die, a few will crop a rich harvest in some other area and leave a lot of surviving offspring as a consequence of their good living.

A similar state of affairs exists on the tundra. This is a tortured land that stretches from the taiga in the south, to the glaciers and Arctic sea in the north. In all, there are five million square miles of this treeless habitat, covered with lichens, mosses, dwarf willows and saxifrages, which hug the ground to escape the cutting polar winds. The winter is long and the summer brief, so that only the top few inches of soil thaw out and the permafrost extends down to at least 700ft(213m) in places. Drainage is virtually non-existent and bogs full of spongy sphagnum moss and glacial litter break up the otherwise featureless landscape. Inhospitable though it may seem, the tundra is the home of the musk ox, reindeer and caribou in Eurasia and North America respectively. They graze on the lichens, taking refuge in the taiga in the winter. Once the tundra was the preferred summer habitat of mammoths, and even now perfectly preserved specimens rise from the permafrost and glaciers like shaggy ghosts.

Waders and wildfowl in millions fly north onto the tundra to breed and it is the hunting ground for polar bears, Arctic foxes, skuas, gyr falcons and the circumpolar yellow-eyed snowy owl. This great white owl is capricious in its appearance and breeding, and

TUNDRA

Snowy owl

Shorteared owl

Lemmings

Snowshoe rabbit

Lynx

NORTH AMERICAN TAIGA

Pygmy owl

Red squirrel

Boreal owl

Great grey owl

NORTHERN
EUROPEAN
TAIGA

Hawk owl

Tengmalm's owl

Great horned owl

Crossbill

Siskin

Some irruption species of the tundra and taiga regions of Northern America and Europe

although its home is among the most desolate of landscapes at the top of the world, it sometimes strikes south into temperate climates. This is solely due to its dependence upon tundra mammals like the collared (*Myodes torquatus*) and common (*Lemmus lemmus*) lemmings, which are rotund little rodents; the latter species is attractively patterned in orange and black. During the wintertime, life carries on normally for the tundra lemmings which dig their way beneath the snow cover by using the horny pads on their feet. Inside their snow tunnels, the microclimate is not nearly so severe and until spring arrives they nibble their way through the mat of vegetation over the ground.

Lemmings are prolific; they have two litters of up to eight each summer, and can breed when they are four or five weeks old, so that when conditions are favourable for reproduction the lemming population can build up quickly to extremely high densities. When this happens, lemmings are thick on the ground and vegetation is rapidly denuded. At this time some of the population becomes nomadic, and lemmings may appear in areas outside their more usual tundra habitats. When lemmings reach plague proportions, predators like short-eared owls and snowy owls settle in high densities to feast on the larger than usual rodent 'cake', and when this happens their breeding season will be marked by more surviving offspring than in average or poor years. Accordingly, there is a population explosion of these birds; but when lemmings are scarce over wide areas, then snowy owls may fail to breed and may erupt from their traditional homelands. Irruptions are particularly noticeable in North America because there is a greater expanse of tundra to the north of that continent as compared with Europe, and so the holding capacity for snowy owls is correspondingly greater. One of the heaviest 'flights' of these big white owls ever to be recorded in the United States occurred in the winter of 1926–7. Altogether, 2,368 observations of snowy owls were received by Dr Alfred Gross, who reviewed the movement, and these were made from as far south as North Carolina, Dakota, Illinois and West Virginia. During such irruptions, snowy owls may intercept ships several hundreds of miles from land, and many have reached the British Isles as non-paying passengers aboard boats ploughing across the North Atlantic.

The mass movement referred to above originated in arctic Canada, and it followed a year when not lemmings but snowshoe rabbits were abundant, and we can conclude that these owls raised big families on the tundras that year. Then a catastrophic decline in the rabbits set thousands of snowy owls searching for food southwards into the USA via the Great Lakes. Flights of snowy owls have been recorded in Europe, too, and individuals have been seen in winter as far south as the Azores. In recent years, Scandinavia has seen irruptions of this species in the winters of 1960 to 1963, and it was at about this time that snowy owls started turning up in the British Isles in unprecedented numbers. Between 1958 and 1962 the Rarities Committee of the British Trust for Ornithology accepted only four records of snowy owls, whereas in the subsequent four years up to 1966 no less than twenty sightings were deemed to be reliable. Then, on the island of Fetlar, one of the Shetland group off the north-east corner of Scotland, a pair of snowy owls eventually bred in 1967, constituting the first authentic record of nesting in the British Isles. Their diet was catholic, and was composed of rabbits but supplemented by bird fare such as oyster catcher and Arctic skua chicks. The Royal Society for the Protection of Birds immediately established a nature reserve and wardens kept a 24-hour vigil daily to keep over-zealous ornithologists and egg collectors at bay. The effort was rewarded in the short term. During a few breeding seasons the VIBs laid 49 eggs and fledged 23 offspring. The original pair of owls nested annually until 1974. In 1973 and the following year, a second hen attached herself to the breeding cock, and in 1975 she was the only fertile female, and managed to rear 4 chicks. Unfortunately the male then vanished for good, leaving a bevy of hens—one was still left in 1988—destined to a barren existence and arousing an earnest debate among the birding community as to the desirability of releasing another cock bird onto Fetlar!

Of course, the breeding range of these great white owls must have oscillated a great deal during the last million years or so, depending upon the advances and retreats of the polar glaciers which have

Barn owl chicks are typically hatched at intervals of a day or two so that the eldest has the best chance of surviving hard times (*Kim Taylor/Bruce Coleman Ltd*)

marked the Pleistocene period. However, we are now somewhere between two ice ages, with a fairly mild climate and a minimal area of tundra, and one can hazard a guess that there are fewer snowy owls living today than perhaps sixteen thousand years ago when the polar ice reached Scotland and northern Ireland. Nevertheless, it is quite possible that, mild though the climate is today, years of successive irruptions have resulted in a temporary extension of the breeding range of the snowy owl to the British Isles. In Russia, mass movements of these birds occur in some years, depending upon the snowfall and food supplies, and flights even reach the Ukraine.

Nomadic opportunist species like the snowy, short-eared and hawk owls on the one hand, and sedentary tawny and great horned owls on the other, are extremes in owl types. Leaving aside the regular migrant ones like the scops, the barn owl falls midway between the two groups. On the continent of Europe, barn owls fluctuate in number and certain years are marked by a more than usually heavy winter death rate. In Holland—a country with about 3,000 breeding pairs—M. R. Honer, working for the State Institute for Nature Conservation Research, studied the causes of these large-scale oscillations in barn owl numbers. Apart from making an analysis of the ornithological literature, the extent of these fluctuations was assessed by summarising the returns of taxidermists, because such is the demand for mounted specimens that many owls pass through their workshops. Taxidermist records show that business was brisk in barn owls in some years more than others; in 1947–8, 488 passed through their hands, between 1950 and '52, 1,130 were mounted (mostly between 1950–1), and in 1953–4 and 1957, 488 and 347 respectively were processed for customers. Birds which had been subjected to postmortems were found to be emaciated, with no fat reserves, and it seemed likely that they had starved to death. High mortality of barn owls had been noted in Holland in 1944, '47, '50, 53, and possibly '58, and the periodicity of 3–5 years was strongly reminiscent of the population cycles of micro-rodents upon which these owls depend.

Blakiston's fish owl is one of the rarest breeding birds in Japan; their normal tactic is to sit and wait, but they sometimes swoop like an osprey (*Steve Kaufman/Bruce Coleman Ltd*)

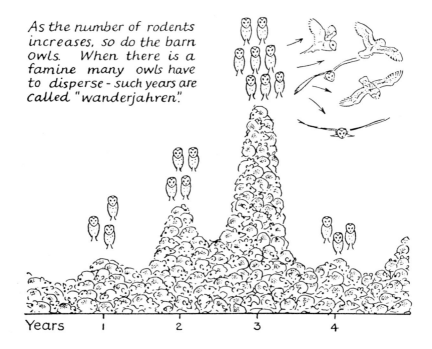

As the number of rodents increases, so do the barn owls. When there is a famine many owls have to disperse - such years are called "wanderjahren".

Years   1   2   3   4

Barn owls, however, have the reputation of being sedentary, but an investigation made by U. Sauter of the recoveries of birds ringed in Germany showed that in certain years barn owls certainly travel far and wide; she called these *Wanderjahren*—'wander years'. In the autumn and winters of 1928–9, 1934–5, 1937–8, 1947–8, 1950–1, and 1952–3, barn owls tended to spread out from their nesting sites and turned up all over Europe. They may even cross the North Sea, because from time to time barn owls of the dark-breasted continental variety (*Tyto alba guttata*) have been recorded in the British Isles. For instance, in the autumn of 1887 and '88, and again ten years later, 'considerable numbers' arrived in Northumberland. Many ended up in taxidermists' windows. In September 1891 a local bird stuffer in Norwich did very well in barn owls because no less than forty were brought in to him. The dispersal during a *Wanderjahr* involves chiefly yearlings birds, although more mature individuals may take part. Very often a period of mass dispersal is accompanied by a high mortality of either older birds (1943–4, 1947–8, 1950–1), or both adults and young (1952–3), or only young birds (1938–9). It was concluded that a combination of two factors lead to a dispersal; a high density of barn owls and a falling density of micro-rodent prey.

In Holland, small rodents have a three-year cycle. The populations build up in the first and second years, reaching a peak during the third summer. As with the tawny owl, breeding may be inhibited if the food supply is very low but, conversely, larger and repeated clutches are the result of an increasing and generous supply. During a peak summer, pairs of barn owls are able to raise perhaps nine young spread over two broods. However, if at the end of the summer and autumn the micro-rodent population goes into a steep decline, then the fledglings must hunt longer and farther away from their parents' territories, and their wanderings may take them hundreds of miles across Europe. If the prey density is much reduced, widespread starvation is bound to occur, both in the remaining adults and their nomadic offspring. In this unhappy situation it will be the lot of many owls to die of exhaustion, and cold spells during the winter will, of course, reduce the chances of emaciated birds surviving until the spring.

Clearly, all owls are faced with varying supplies of food and yet several quite different ways of life have evolved for them which have survival value for their adherents in their own particular habitats. Nomadism is clearly vital to species whose food supply fluctuates wildly from year to year and from place to place. Owls like the short-eared and snowy are obviously able to exploit prey wherever it occurs, and as populations of these nomadic species are on the move outside the nesting season they will tend to accumulate in numbers that bear some direct relationship to the density of their prey. Despite the fact that woodland species like the tawny owl face similar problems of food shortage, they lead sedentary existences and their chances of survival seem to be better if they remain in their territories. The reason may be this: tawny owls are able to hunt successfully even in bad mouse years because they know every inch of the ground. They have to, because their home territory is so much more complicated than the open moorland, tundra or grassland favoured by short-eared or snowy owls. An acre of moorland is much the same anywhere, but woodlands with their patchwork of scrub and streams, and canopies supported by great trunks, present difficulties for the hunter. A sure knowledge of the terrain will bring dividends. In order to live well in woodland a tawny owl must learn where moles tend to forge their way beneath the leaf litter, and which trees yield rich harvests of nuts for furtive little rodents to gather beneath. Learning the geography takes time, and the starving owl may not have time on its side. For the tawny owl, faced with famine conditions, its best bet is to stay at home on familar ground because it is likely to know just where the few remaining mice or voles may be taken; whereas for the short-eared owl, survival is best ensured by moving off to fresh hunting grounds where voles may be plentiful. The barn owl's habitat is midway between open grassland and woodland, and it is interesting that it behaves somewhere between the short-eared and tawny owls; although basically sedentary, barn owl populations will under certain circumstances disperse, thereby resembling the taiga- or tundra-living owls.

We are now in a position to answer the question posed at the beginning of this chapter: what determines the size of owl populations under natural conditions? The fortunes of owls are clearly related closely to those of their prey. When food is abundant then owls grow fat, they are fruitful and indeed multiply. Their clutches are large and the number of young they are able to rear is high, and the owl population increases. This happy state of affairs rarely continues for long because the availability of prey varies from year to year. These fluctuations are not so great in temperate, deciduous woodlands, but reach staggering proportions in the relatively simple taiga and tundra environments where controls and checks upon animal and plant fertility seem to be minimal. In years of famine, owls tend not to breed, or will lay small clutches from which, even if they are not deserted, fewer owlets survive. Some species may then become more nomadic than usual with the chance of finding food elsewhere. In any event, there may be heavy mortality even of adults, and so the owl population declines.

The question naturally arises as to whether owls bring about their own downfall by breeding too bountifully in good micro-rodent years, thereby exhausting the resource upon which they themselves ultimately depend. The burden of evidence indicates that the prey species tend to control the number of hunters and not vice versa. The Craigheads, to whom reference has already been made, calculated that only 24% of all the major prey animals were killed by raptors during the winter of 1941–2. They reckoned that this level of predation was sufficient to prevent excessive increase in the prey species but was not severe enough to cause the catastrophic crash in the micro-rodent populations that often follow plague years.

Recent investigations in Finland have confirmed the relatively small pressure exerted by predatory birds upon the hugely fecund rodents. Over a 20 square kilometre study area, 40 pairs of nesting short-eared owls were estimated to have consumed 38,000 voles between mid-April and the end of July. With about 350 voles to the hectare during peak years, it meant that the owls were accounting for a mere 5% of the total population.

When the impact of other vole killers was taken into account, the chances still seemed to be in the rodents' favour. In a larger patch of Finland (63km²), 95 nests of predatory birds were discovered by E. Korpimaki and his collaborators. They belonged to 33 pairs of short-eared, 21 long-eared, 2 Tengmalm's owls, as well as to 36 pairs of kestrels and 3 pairs of hen harriers. The biologists calculated that the birds of prey needed 64cwt(3,252kg) of food, and that this probably amounted to 83,000 microtus voles, 13,000 bank voles, 4,500 shrews and 2,500 small birds. A further calculation based upon trapping results pointed to the fact that there were about 378,000 microtus voles available to the avian predators, thus revealing that the owls and raptors were only cropping 22% of the resource — or just under one in five rodents. In other words, it seems unlikely that owls and hawks eat themselves out of business.

An explanation for these fluctuations must probably be traced farther back along the food chains. The rodents themselves might exhaust their own food supplies, whether they be hazel nuts or grasses in the case of the lemmings and voles. Furthermore, the normal social behaviour of these small rodents may change in response to overcrowding, and this in itself may result in a widespread breeding failure with a consequential population drop. When this happens, the predators will suffer because the high level of the food supply to which they have adapted will, over the course of a few months, dwindle to meagre proportions. The fortunes of the hunter are ironically not so much in the lap of the gods, but inextricably tied up with the fortunes of the hunted.

But man and the march of civilisation have affected the history of owls in many diverse ways—some good and some bad.

4 *Owls and Man*

In the last chapter an attempt was made to consider some of the 'natural' circumstances which have a bearing upon the numbers of owls. From the preceding pages, it will have been gathered that nature is rarely simple, that all animals strike up relationships with others, and that the fortunes or misfortunes of one can have far-reaching repercussions on others in the 'jigsaw'. Man enters the picture because the impact of this busy, enterprising ape upon the landscape over the last ten thousand years has been so utterly fundamental that his influence upon nearly all living things, including owls, cannot be ignored.

Man served a very long apprenticeship as a hunter, extracting a living from collecting fruits and cropping game animals. He must have been, as indeed hunters are today, a keen and sensitive observer of wildlife, and the beautiful rock and cave paintings of animals in Europe and Africa bear witness to this. The pictorial legacy left to us by Palaeolithic peoples in Europe shows that at that time the paths of man and owl had already crossed. At Trois Frères, in France, the unmistakable outline of a pair of snowy owls and their chicks is chipped out of a rock face; the artist lived at a time when the Arctic glaciers extended farther south than today and rendered much of France suitable as breeding grounds for these owls.

Snowy owls were not only considered as birds of beauty, worthy of an artist's attention, but they were also appreciated gastronomically, as the presence of their scraped bones on Neolithic dwelling sites indicates. Even today Eskimos still eat them. In those far-off days man must have been a rare species which, like any other predator, had to come to terms with its prey. There would have been little need for a Stone Age equivalent of the World Wildlife Fund; for, to have over-exploited a food supply at that time would have spelt disaster. Man, however, was never just like an ordinary predator because he had the potential to mould and alter the environment to suit his immediate needs, irrespective of whether these were necessarily in his long-term interests. Tools and fire became part of his working equipment, and never before in the history of this planet had an animal had such power to alter the face of the world, particularly when the skills of stock-breeding and cultivation had been developed. Easily obtained food surpluses then allowed increased survival for men and their families. The population explosion, which may culminate in something like 7,000 million souls by the year AD 2000, had its origins 10,000 years BC.

The impact of man on owl populations is mixed, and it might be useful at this stage to consider a few of the effects that the advance of civilisation had on owls in the British Isles and other parts of Europe. Although men have, on the whole, been hewers of wood, planters of cereals and builders of towns and cities, none of these activities has, in itself, been disastrous for owls.

After the last glaciation, before man dominated the scene, it can be surmised that the tawny owl was the commonest species on the mainland of Britain, as it is today, and lived in the widespread deciduous forests that flourished in the warm, moist climate. Long-eared owls probably took over in the pine forests of the north, as well as in Ireland, where they still flourish in the absence of tawnies today. It has always been popularly held that St Patrick cleaned up

Tawny owls roost during the day, but enjoy sunbathing (*W.C. Wilkes/Aquila Photographics*)

Ireland as part and parcel of his missionary work, banishing such evil animals as toads, snakes and, presumably, a host of birds which are now missing from the Irish countryside. Colourful though the theory is, the residential tawny owl was prevented from colonising what is now Ireland by the formation of the Irish Sea perhaps 8,000 years ago, when it, along with many other animals, was slowly regaining lost ground in the wake of the retreating ice. The tawny must have entered the mainland of England before the English Channel opened up in about 5000 BC. The Irish Sea, nevertheless, proved no barrier to the more nomadic or migrant long-eared, short-eared and barn owls. However, in those far-off days, man and owl must only occasionally have come face to face.

Then events took place in the Near and Middle East which revolutionised the situation and brought man and owl more closely together. Some time around 8000 BC, local cereals, including wheat and barley, were domesticated. The agricultural revolution had started, and by the second millennium before Christ, great areas over the whole of Europe had been converted to growing these highly productive crops. Trees made way for grasses, and as man's population rose, more land was needed to produce food; the axe was kept busy for thousands of years. Today, only four out of fifty-six million acres of Britain are woodland—nearly a quarter of it coniferous—whereas well over half of the total is under crops and grass. Of course, this revolution in land use took place over thousands of years in Britain and the rest of Europe, and the effect upon the wildlife was correspondingly slow. But in North America, the settlers, backed by the mass-produced steel axes of Elisha King Root, decimated the indigenous forests in a hundred years or so and the effect of this upon barred, great gray, saw-whet and great horned owls must have been catastrophic in terms of the sizes of their populations.

In Britain and much of Europe, the gradual destruction of the primeval woodlands to make way for agriculture must have reduced the numbers of tawny owls, but the changes probably favoured the spread of a species that preferred hunting over wet meadows, grassland strips, or along the outskirts of woods within a stone's throw of secure, dry shelters—the cosmopolitan barn owl.

Of all birds, the barn owl is very dependent upon human activity, and, in the British Isles, the history of our relationship with these beautiful birds can be traced back at least two millennia. Their bones have been excavated on the site of the Iron Age lake village of Glastonbury, in Somerset. The pre-Roman inhabitants of this sophisticated society of potters and weavers were doubtless familiar with these ghostly white owls and may even have enjoyed them as a dish, along with young Dalmation pelicans, a species long since vanished from our wetlands. Barn owls were also known to the peoples of another lake village in County Meath, in Ireland, which flourished nearly a thousand years later, between AD 750 and 950. Clearly the creation of meadows and pastures, the growing of cereals and the construction of dwelling places suited barn owls far more at that stage than any other owl.

Seeds have always been the staple diet of most rodents, and wherever we have planted and stored cereals rodents have flourished, thus benefiting owls and other small predators. House mice the world over are probably descended from a wild sub-species (*Mus musculus wagneri*) which lives in the dry steppe lands of northern Iran and Turkestan, where the first agricultural settlements have been found. From here, mice followed the grain into North Africa, Europe and to the New World, making a thorough nuisance of themselves by destroying valuable stores and spreading disease. It is not surprising that the Egyptians made a sacred animal of the cat, and four thousand years later the pioneer farmers in North America likewise held the cat in high esteem. Perhaps, too, the good work of owls might have been acknowledged! In North America, gophers are a menace to crops, but perhaps the most successful rodent to have plagued man is the brown rat, which reached the British Isles between 1728 and 1730, probably hitching a lift on ships from Persia. It has been a persistent pest to crops and has multiplied around farms. Today, the diet of barn owls living around farms is made up of up to 60 per cent by weight of this introduced rodent, and in California pouched gophers comprise their favourite food. House mice seem to be less important as a source of food, but the short-tailed voles, which must have profited enormously from the creation of meadows and pastures, are perhaps the largest single item on the menu for these owls.

The food supply for the barn owl was thus assured by the growing of cereal crops and, through the Enclosures Acts, by the development of meadows and pastures; the farm buildings containing straw-bedded cattle and with lofts and crevices, ventilation shafts, chimney stacks, or the village church belfries, made fine substitutes as nesting and roosting places for cavities in trees or, especially, rock faces. Because of their prowess at catching rats, voles, and mice around the granaries and hayricks, the snoring and screeching of these tenants were familiar and tolerated. (John of Guildford, in his classic poem 'The Owl and the Nightingale', called the barn owl 'the owl that schrichest', as opposed to the owl that 'yollest'—the tawny.) Even the name testifies to the close association between farmer and owl, at least in England; indeed some very old barns have in-built nest boxes which are open invitations to owl couples. In the Netherlands, where it goes by the name of 'church owl' (*kervil*), farmer and owl were friends, and Friesland farmers have for long encouraged these silent hunters of the hated rats and mice, even to the extent of building access routes into the lofts and roof spaces in their houses. Large Friesean farmhouses often show a decorative complex called an 'owl board' (*oeleboerd*) on the front of the roof ridge, with a round opening in the centre called the 'owl hole' (*oelegat*). Strangely enough, nests are rarely made in inhabited houses, but once the occupants have left, barn owls quickly take over and make a nursery of the upper storeys.

Man and owl formed a tolerably happy relationship for centuries, and perhaps in the Middle Ages, when woodlands were reduced to their lowest point in history because of the demand for timber and charcoal, the barn owl was the most abundant species. Indeed, one British chronicler wrote in 1781 that the 'white owl' was 'very common in most of the European countries and none more so than this Kingdom'. But that happy state of affairs was not to continue.

Over the past two hundred years, the relationship between barn owls and people has become ever more tarnished as a result of changes in land use ushered in by the eighteenth century. As a consequence, the population of these much-cherished birds has been in a state of constant and often dramatic change. The first proper national census took place in 1932 when George Blaker made a pioneering attempt to establish the status of the species for the Royal Society for the Protection of Birds. Using information from between 50 and 100 birdwatchers, and utilizing data collected from 4,000 others, he concluded that there were only 25,000 barn owls left in

Barn owl, *Tyto alba*. This beautiful species is comparatively rare in certain areas; feeding mainly on rodents, it is a good friend to the farmer and is specifically protected by law (*D. Ruane*)

the United Kingdom (12,000 pairs and 1,000 unattached birds). Furthermore, he reckoned the species was declining. Today, only one third of this number of barn owls survives in our countryside. A host of factors conspired against them, not least the misguided and over-zealous 'predator controlling' activities of gamekeepers who regarded any mammal with well-developed canine teeth, or bird with hooked bill and talons, as worthy of nothing more than immediate liquidation. The effects of game management on owls will be mentioned more fully later on, but it is sufficient to say here that, even today, a few owls, the barn and tawny included, fall victims to cruel and illegal pole traps. Barn owls were probably particularly vulnerable to persecution because they often roost in places close to human habitation, and their hunting method of quartering the ground, combined with their overall pale coloration, makes them conspicuous targets.

The upsurge of gamekeeping was by no means the only cause of the barn owl's ceasing to be one of the most, if not the most, numerous owls in the British Isles. Fundamental changes were taking place in the organisation of farming. Horsepower was giving way to tractors; great draught horses were no longer around the farms spilling grain upon which small rodents flourished. Farms were becoming cleaner and neater, and crops were being stored in places where they were safe from mice and rats. Gone are the days when cereal crops were reaped by binders and the sheaves collected into stacks for threshing at a later date. Those were halcyon times for farmyard rodents, when grain was spilt literally into the mouths of hosts of hungry and fertile mice, voles, and rats. So, with fewer potential nest-sites, and a reduced population of scavenging rodents, owls were being put out of business. Even village church towers, traditionally places for owls and bats, were being wired up to discourage noisy lodgers like jackdaws and feral pigeons from contributing to the Sunday services, and the more deserving owls suffered in consequence.

Habitat changes, too, may well have contributed to their general decline. Barn owls have always preferred hunting over rough pastures, hedgerows and hayricks, and with the general 'tidying up' of the countryside tens of thousands of acres of good barn owl land have been made unsuitable for them. The plough has been drawn across pastures where field voles once flourished. Damp meadows or wetlands over which barn owls used to hunt beneath the moon have been drained. Machines have been getting larger, and big machines require big fields for economical operation. 95% of our permanent hay meadows have disappeared under the plough largely in favour of barley, but to the detriment of barn owls. Hedgerows, a relatively recent innovation brought about by the Enclosures Acts but hugely beneficial to wildlife, have been falling before the bulldozers at a colossal rate. In 1961, there were 616,000 miles (985,280km) of hedges in Great Britain, but an estimated 125,000 miles (202,323km) of this favourable habitat have been grubbed up since the last war. We may still be losing 2,000 miles (3,219km) of this valuable reservoir for animals and plants annually. Little and barn owls have already suffered from the onslaught of the bulldozers, and even the burgeoning traffic problem has not left owls unscathed since both species are killed in numbers on the roads; 5,000 barn owls are doomed to die on roadside verges each year. And to this miserable record of modern-day factors which operate against the barn owl in the British Isles must now be added a far more insidious one.

Since the end of the Second World War there has been what can only be called a serious decline of nearly all birds of prey, not only in the British Isles but also in North America and over much of Europe. Of the owls, the barn owl has suffered most. At the beginning of the century, the county of Essex, bordering London, had one of the densest populations, estimated at between 41 and 50 per 100 square miles. Since the area of Essex is 1,528 square miles, there were presumably between 700 and 800 pairs of barn owls in those days, hunting around the spinneys and hayricks. This figure had dropped to about 500 pairs by the 1932 census, but today the number of breeding pairs has fallen to less than 100 pairs in this county. The onset of this latter downward trend in population corresponds to their marked disappearance from many traditional habitats in the 1950s, when agricultural pesticides were being brought into widespread use in an attempt to control the ravages of pests, thereby squeezing every pound of food from the soil. These were not banned in the UK until 1974. However, the decline of ramshackle farm buildings used for roosting and nesting, the reduction of grasslands upon which rodents thrived, and the ever-increasing mortality due to road traffic were all contributory causes of the barn owl's demise.

Ringing has proved a useful tool in substantiating the decline of the barn owl in the British Isles. For example, if figures for the numbers of nestlings ringed each year are analysed from the end of the Second World War, it will be found that those for the barn owl, expressed as a percentage of the total for all species, has reduced from about 0.2 to between 0.05 and 0.01 in 1963–4. This comes at a time when the number of bird-ringers was increasing prodigiously. By comparison, the 'catch' of kestrels showed no significant trends either upwards or downwards and fluctuated according to the abundance of its main prey—short-tailed field voles.

Tawny owls throughout the post-war period have been remarkable for showing hardly any change of status, and it is possible that their preference for hunting inside woodlands has left them compar-

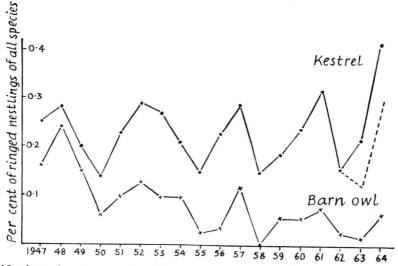

Numbers of nestling kestrels and barn owls ringed annually in Britain and Ireland, 1947–64, expressed as a percentage of the annual totals of ringed nestlings of all species. Because of a national survey into its status, special attention was paid to the kestrel in 1963 and 1964, and the dotted line may better indicate the extent of the fluctuation in these two years compared with previous ones. Redrawn from Parslow 1967 with the permission of the author and the editors of *British Birds*

atively immune to the chronic effects of crop sprays. Barn owls, because their hunting flyways are often over fields, have taken the full brunt of this revolution in agricultural management.

By far the worst offending chemicals to take their place in the farmer's armoury against disease and the pestilence in his crops have been the organo-chlorines, of which DDT was one of the first and best known. DDT was synthesized in the laboratory in 1874, but its insecticidal properties were not discovered until 1939. The beneficial effect of DDT on human diseases like louse-borne typhus and malaria cannot be underestimated. But after the war this chlorinated hydro-carbon became more widely used as a crop insecticide; in the United States, for example, it was used against the beetle that promotes Dutch Elm disease, and against pine-looper caterpillars. And once the environment became contaminated, wildlife began to suffer.

DDT is a poison with special properties; for a start, it is a fairly persistent chemical which remains in the soil, and in living tissues, for a great length of time. In large enough quantities it affects the nervous system, causing the spontaneous firing off of nerves, which leads, in turn, to acute convulsions and death. Animals vary in their sensitivity to it; residues of the order of 100 or less parts per million may be associated with death in birds, whereas brine shrimps may be killed by three weeks' exposure to sea water contaminated by one part per million million ($1 : 10^{12}$). In sub-lethal doses, it leads to atypical behaviour but, what is just as important, the body's chemical machinery has, it seems, only limited means of detoxifying and excreting it. As DDT and other organo-chlorines are highly soluble in fat, small doses accumulate in the liver, or fat tissues, until perhaps starvation or stress causes the accumulated dose to be released over a very short period, as the fats are needed (eg, during migration or in the winter). Once DDT has become dissolved in living tissue, it is quickly passed up the food chain and tends to become concentrated in predators.

In recent years it has been discovered that DDT interferes with the production of the sex hormones—testosterone, oestrogen, and progesterone—and this might account for the widespread breeding failure among birds of prey, which has been particularly noticeable in the peregrine. Increased or depressed levels of oestrogen synthesis can lead to abnormalities in calcium transport around the body,

which is so necessary for egg formation. Egg breaking has been on
the increase in the post-war years, and recently Dr Derek Ratcliffe,
of the Nature Conservancy's Experimental Station at Monks Wood,
in England, has found that in the period since 1947 practically the
whole population of peregrines in Britain produced eggs, the shells
of which were thinner by 18 per cent than those of eggs laid before
1947. Apart from the possibility that poisoned birds might themselves
show aberrant behaviour, the lighter-shelled eggs are almost certainly
weaker and therefore break more easily. Eggshells of North American
peregrines have also been shown to have undergone a thinning of
about 18 per cent since 1947, and a similar phenomenon has been
demonstrated to have occurred in several other kinds of birds of
prey, in both Britain and North America. Breeding failure due to
thin-shelled eggs is no idle speculation. Even fish-eaters pick up

organo-chlorines through the food chain; brown pelicans failed to nest in California in 1969 because their eggs just collapsed beneath the adults as they tried to incubate them. It is possible then that the same phenomenon might be found in barn owls.

By the early 1950s, a new class of chemicals related to DDT became available to the farmer to combat pests, and among these dieldrin perhaps turned out to be even more destructive to wildlife. Wheat dressed with dieldrin to combat the ravages of the wheat-bulb fly is usually sown in the autumn, when it does comparatively little damage to wildlife. However, between 1956 and 1961, large kills of seed-eating birds and raptors occurred in the cereal-growing areas of the British Isles, following the spring sowing of dieldrin-dressed grain. Some incidents involving the poisoning of thousands of woodpigeons were reported; pheasants and foxes, too, were recorded as dying in unusually large numbers. During the autumn, food is plentiful and freshly-sown grain is hardly touched, but in spring, after the lean months at the end of the winter, there is great competition for whatever food is available. Wheat, dieldrin and all, is taken by rodents and seed-eating birds alike, and these quickly become convulsive and moribund, so that they fall easy prey to the predators.

As little as ten parts of dieldrin per million in the tissues of a kestrel is enough to kill it, and this could easily be picked up from eating seven poisoned voles within a short period. A sparrowhawk might not survive after eating three greenfinches that had been feeding upon the dressed grain, and a peregrine need only take three contaminated pigeons to kill it. Now, it had always been assumed that the decline of birds of prey had been due to the slow build-up of organo-chlorines in their tissues, by eating otherwise healthy but slightly contaminated prey, and that this led, first, to infertility, followed later by death. However, the sudden drop in the numbers of the sparrowhawk and peregrine over a period of a few years has tended to support the idea that these insecticides produce their effect through a few incidents of gross poisoning of adults, whose replacement is hindered by widespread breeding failure of the remaining population.

The impetus of the agro-chemical industry continues to be a threat to owls as farmers add yet more noxious compounds to their armoury against pests. Rodenticides like Warfarin which prevent the blood from clotting pose the latest danger. Grain dowsed in these deadly products causes the victims to bleed to death. Mice and rats can pass on the poison should they in turn fall prey to owls or other raptors. Warfarin was one of the first rodenticides on the market with a relatively low toxicity because it breaks down quickly in the body. However, the so-called second generation of anti-coagulants is devastatingly lethal. For instance, Difenacoum and Brodefacoum are 100 and 600 times respectively more toxic than Warfarin. Two mice poisoned with either of these products would be sufficient to kill an owl. If used properly, the risks to predatory creatures should be minimal but, unfortunately, some farmers are tempted to ply the deadly bait by hedgerows to catch rodents on their way to and from the farm buildings, and this is where the owls tend to patrol.

In Sweden, mercury has reached dangerous levels particularly in the lakes. Sweden has a history of using mercury compounds in its wood pulp industries, as well as of applying alkyl-mercury substances as seed dressings since the 1940s. As a poison, mercury is particularly pernicious because it builds up in the body and becomes localised in the brain. Attention was drawn to this contamination in Sweden by the widespread deaths of birds, and to unduly high levels of mercury in fish; as much as two parts per million were found in some salmon. Predatory species tend to accumulate persistent elements from their food, and so eagles, owls, and hawks, together with grain-feeding pheasants and partridges, were looked at in detail to see just how widespread the contamination was.

One of the first facts to be established was how long this element had been building up in the country, so that the origins of the mercury sources could be pin-pointed beyond reasonable doubt. As it happens, both sea eagles and eagle owls were very useful in providing the Swedes with a long-term picture of the mercury pollution over the last hundred years because this element is deposited in the feathers as they are being rapidly built up during the moult period. The extent to which mercury is incorporated in the feathers depends upon how fast they grow and how much poison is taken in with the food, and this bears a direct relationship to the level of environmental contamination. Each feather is, therefore, an indicator of the amount of mercury around at the time it was being formed.

In order to monitor the levels of mercury over a long period, Swedish scientists turned to museum specimens of birds of prey, and when analyses were made of their feathers it was discovered that the feathers' mercury content stayed more or less constant in specimens of the same species for a century, from 1840 to 1940. Then over the next ten years, up until 1950, there was a ten- to twenty-fold increase, at a time when alkyl-mercury seed dressings were being used on a massive scale. Eagle owl tail feathers contained up to 2.5 parts of mercury per million before 1933, but later on the astonishingly high amount of forty-one parts per million was found in the feathers of a breeding individual. Even so, this figure was insignificant when compared with analyses of sea eagles, which were up to sixty-four parts per million, and these birds feed on freshwater fish which might have accumulated as much as fourteen parts per million in their tissues. After feeding on several contaminated fish, the eagles would perhaps have soon accumulated enough mercury in their own bodies to make them sterile.

In 1967 the Public Health Institute, a Swedish government establishment, came to the conclusion that fish containing more than one part per million of mercury were unfit for human consumption, although as more evidence came to light a ban was introduced on the sale of fish from *waters* where a mercury level of one part per million was found. With the Swedish fishing industry thus threatened, there was a considerable tightening up of the use of organo-mercury compounds in Sweden. Even organo-chlorines came under the scrutiny of the National Poisons and Pesticides Board, which has the power to license the use of agricultural and domestic preparations in Sweden. As from 1 January 1970, even DDT was banished from domestic use for a trial period of two years, because of the evidence building up against that widespread insecticide. Sweden also pressed the United Nations into sponsoring an international conference on environmental pollution for 1972.

It is doubtful if any kinds of owl suffered through pesticides in Sweden as much as their relatives in England, although the barn owl is at its northernmost limits in Scandinavia, and toxic chemicals might be expected to hit the sparse population harder in that region than in areas where life is inherently easier for them.

Following in Sweden's footsteps, there was a great awakening to the dangers of environmental pollution in advanced countries. 'To be concerned about pollution is very U—very fashionable,' stated Tom Dalyell, a member of the British House of Commons, writing in the *New Scientist* on 1 January 1970—and about time, too, most enlightened thinkers would add. But the problem facing administrators was, and still is, a tricky one. Industry and pollution go to a large extent hand in hand with rising living standards to which governments are rightly committed. Certainly, the environment with all its animals and plants can be protected, but there need to be some very radical changes in society first. The fact must be faced that in the short term it is cheaper to pollute the air, sea, and rivers, and to blanket the land and crops with fertilisers, fungicides, insecticides and a host of other chemicals that help to produce bumper crops to feed the millions. So, in the long run, it seems likely that everyone will have to dig deeply into their pockets to pay for their rights to a clean, wholesome world.

The first moves were made towards that Utopian ideal when DDT was outlawed in the United States, while in the British Isles, in addition to a voluntary ban on spring-sown dressed seeds, the Wilson Report on DDT recommended a reduction in the use of this chemical, although many would have been happier had the government resolved to replace organo-chlorine pesticides by 1971 with less harmful compounds.

Canada and New Zealand, too, were attacking the problem, and their efforts, together with those already mentioned, were the first welcome moves towards what one can only hope will become a world-wide campaign to reduce pollutants and to prevent excessive use of fertilisers and persistent poisons such as DDT; because once these chemicals have entered the biosphere, they will turn up on everyone's doorstep. All credit must go to organisations like the Royal Society for the Protection of Birds in the British Isles, and in North America to the late Rachel Carson whose sensitively-written book, *Silent Spring*, brought out into the open the fact that the world was, and still is, being slowly poisoned. So, by the 1970s, the first faltering steps were being taken to treat the countryside and its resources with respect, and it was heartening to learn that, for the first time in perhaps two decades, peregrines were again beginning to breed successfully and to increase in numbers in the British Isles. Perhaps, too, the barn owl will once again 'scritch' in restored numbers around the farmlands, with encouragement from the farmer. However, the deathly pollution of Lake Erie, and the invasion of oil companies into the wilderness of Alaska, give no room for complacency, and the scandalous treatment of air and water alike as media for the disposal of waste matter should inspire us to construct a sensible strategy for the better use of the world's natural resources in the future.

Because of man's ability to produce increasing surpluses of food, more and more people have been able to leave the land and find their living in towns and cities. These, in consequence, have been spreading to engulf the surrounding countryside at a prodigious rate. In the United States of America alone, two acres of the countryside fall beneath bricks and mortar every minute. In Europe, it has been prophesied that there will be a continuous conurbation sprawling between Manchester and Milan. To those who cherish the dream of a pastoral paradise, reflected in the writings of the eighteenth-century parson-naturalist, Gilbert White, or the paintings of John Constable, the subtopias of the twentieth century are considered no better than cancers of asphalt and concrete. The sweet songs of birds are giving way to the dawn chorus of cars speeding sleepy commuters to their desks and computers. At least, this is a popularly held notion, but must towns and cities necessarily be biological deserts?

Man so often creates surroundings which, because they do not adequately meet his psychological needs for freedom and space, he comes to regard as urban hells, yet these same environments, more often than not, furnish food supplies, nesting sites and tolerable privacy for a multitude of birds which go unnoticed in the humdrum of city life. To house sparrows, starlings, house martins, and the grubby descendants of rock doves, eaves and spaces between the tiles are pleasant and adequate substitutes for their originally preferred home sites of overhangs, cliff ledges and rock-strewn slopes. Cities might still be polluted, even by organo-chlorines perhaps sprayed on to gaily decorated window-boxes, but there is no doubt that our throw-away societies are proving to be very acceptable to wild life. Rubbish tips are a godsend to scavenging gulls and foxes alike. Reservoirs and park lakes are suitable for wildfowl; add to this the strong tendency for people to feed birds, and it becomes evident that for birds which can adapt themselves to it, life is good in the suburbs—apart from the traffic, and the cats, of which there are almost half a million in London alone.

The late Kenneth Allsop pointed out that, although we choose to think of the inner zone of cities as asphalt jungle, it is almost as much jungle as asphalt. There are always cemeteries, gardens, parks, derelict weed-covered sites, railway embankments, allotments and the trees that line so many roads. Four large royal parks in London total 1,308 acres, and in one of them, Regents Park, 125 pairs of blackbirds and thirty-seven pairs of song thrushes took up residence one recent summer. To those who are eternally pessimistic of nature's ability to make the best of whatever opportunities arise, it may come as a surprise to learn that towns hold some of the densest populations of birds. The variety may be reduced but, even so, there may be four or five birds to each acre in some areas of London, and the overall breeding density of between one and two pairs per acre is higher than the figures for most types of farmland. The total population of birds in Inner London, for example, is probably between 23,000 and 45,000 pairs, consisting chiefly of house sparrows and feral pigeons.

With such a huge potential supply of food, it is no wonder that towns and cities have their complement of owls, and of all those which have best adapted to suburban life the tawny is clearly the most successful. The owl of London, for example, has always been the tawny, and led Alfred Noyes, the eighteenth-century poet, to write evocatively of:

The linnet and the throstle, too, and after dark the long haloo,
And golden-eyed tu-whit, tu-whoo, of owls that ogle London.

One suspects that although Noyes might often have been 'ogled' by tawny owls, he had rarely 'ogled' them himself, otherwise he would surely have described their eyes as anything but 'golden', if we are to take his lines literally. However, the loud and clear 'haloo' of these birds, arguing out their territorial disputes from parks, cemeteries and roadside trees in spring and autumn, is a common enough experience for most town dwellers, particularly since the beginning of this century when tawnys have been on the increase, following

Tawny owl, *Strix aluco (Eric Hosking)*

their nineteenth-century decline as the result of over-enthusiastic gamekeeping. It is now perhaps Britain's most numerous, and therefore most successful, bird of prey, with an estimated population of 100,000 pairs in the British Isles. Some of these are town owls, but the interesting point is that in order to make a living in their urban surroundings these expert rodent-catchers have had to change their diet. The city tawny owl has become a bird-catcher, snatching pigeons and sparrows from their roosts and even haunting bird tables, where patience is inevitably rewarded. In Holland Park, a part of Inner London, an analysis carried out on tawny owl pellets showed that 93 per cent of the prey units (see Chapter 3) were birds; only 7 per cent were mammals, but the proportion of mammal prey rose with increasing distance from the centre of London (18 per cent at Stockwell, 55 per cent at Morden) until it reached 90 per cent on the outskirts at Bookham Common.

Tawny owls are not the only predatory birds to take up town life. A survey carried out by members of the London Natural History Society over an area of 1,255sq miles (3,255) square kilometres within twenty miles of St Paul's Cathedral revealed that the kestrel was the commonest, with a possible 142 pairs breeding, that is one pair to 8.7sq miles (22.9km²), which compares favourably with the density of kestrels on farmland. The tawny owl was shown to be the next most abundant bird of prey, with forty-eight pairs widely distributed within the region. There was one breeding record from Regents Park. At least forty-nine young were reared from twenty-seven nests (1.8 per nest), which is a good level of productivity for tawny owls, even in their British woodland homes. A similar story of urbanised owls could be repeated for other towns and cities on the mainland of the British Isles. As this chapter is being written, tawny owls are hooting on a golfcourse bounded by busy roads and houses within the city boundary of Bristol, and one of us remembers frequently seeing a tawny owl dodging the evening traffic and cinema queues in the centre of Colchester, more often than not clutching a struggling blackbird or house sparrow screaming away its last moments. During the Second World War, fire-watchers in England used to be familiar with the shadows of tawnies hunting vermin along the streets and bomb sites.

The patchwork of high-rise building, parks and suburbia clearly does not suit barn owls, the more surprisingly perhaps since these have long shacked down with us in farms and villages. Even so, a few pairs have established themselves precariously in places. Within 20 miles (32km) of St Paul's Cathedral, seven pairs were recorded in London in 1967, and most of these preferred the open country towards the outer limits of the area covered by the survey. One pair reared five owlets in a chestnut tree in Kempton Park, which they shared with a couple of kestrels and their family of four. Dulwich, Osterly Park, Beddington and Barking are all built-up London suburban areas and all have their 'white owls', but none had ventured into Inner London. When barn owls do breed in towns, they tend to hit the headlines; the *Daily Express* for Wednesday, 30 October 1968 reported 'Murder in Romford'; 'Terror lurks at night among the rustling trees and dew-covered grasses of an Essex park'. A lone Scotland Yard sleuth, we were told, had been on the trail for two months watching each time the assassin returned home with a victim. The killers, of course, were a pair of barn owls nesting in a broken elm tree near the home of a police photographer, and the victims were voles, mice, rats and birds.

Little and long-eared owls occasionally turn up in towns, but never in such numbers as to rival their larger cousin, the tawny. Around the Mediterranean, the tiny scops owl could almost be called a town owl because it often takes up residence in trees lining the roads, and early in spring the bell-like notes of the cock form part of the busy night-time chorus of crickets and cicadas. Street lamps, hotel signs and lighted windows may attract night-flying moths and insects, and the scops owl has probably learned to associate the electric landscape of man with easy pickings.

In North America, screech owls are regular residents in townships and city parks, and the smaller hawk owls frequent the Australian suburbs. To the north, the syncopated hoots of the Ural owl are a familiar sound to town dwellers in Asia.

City owls must surely be welcomed by most people who are not worried by any of the numerous superstitions associated with those who hear their melancholy hoots. They may, however, be a slight menace in the breeding season when they become particularly bold in defending their nest sites. Owls have, however, been discouraged

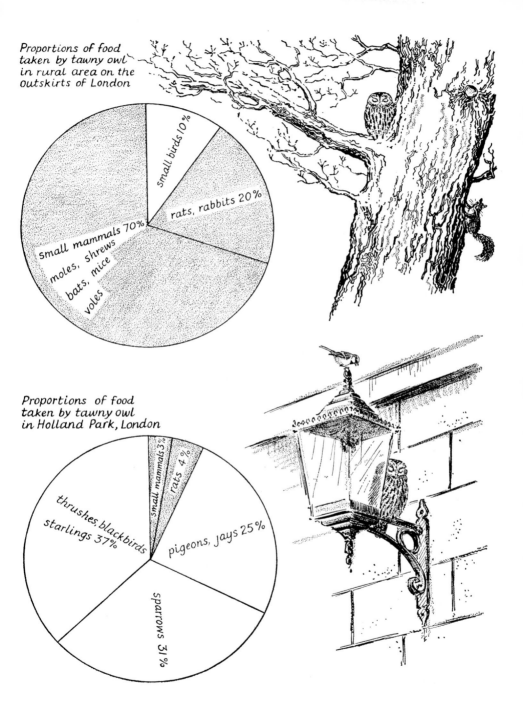

Proportions of food
taken by tawny owl
in rural area on the
outskirts of London

small birds 10%

rats, rabbits 20%

small mammals 70%
moles, shrews
bats, mice
voles

Proportions of food
taken by tawny owl
in Holland Park, London

thrushes, blackbirds
starlings 37%

small mammals 3%

rats 4%

pigeons, jays 25%

sparrows 31%

from living on airfields in Canada, where these birds proved to be a direct threat to human life through risk of collision with aircraft. It cannot, however, be pretended that these birds are uppermost in the league of species which give most cause for concern in this respect; gulls are by far the biggest culprits, but in Canada, snowy, great horned, and short-eared owls were all involved in 'strikes'. Canada, because of its wetlands near to the airports, used to suffer greatly from bird strike hazards, and in the sixties at least five CF-104 type of aircraft crashed after colliding with birds. Taken as a whole, that country's commercial airlines recorded over 1,000 strikes at a direct cost of two million dollars, and that amount of money was spent by the Royal Canadian Air Force between 1961 and 1963. Bulletin No 5 of the Associate Committee on Bird Hazards to Aircraft reported that, in 1966, there were 4.35 strikes for every 100,000 take-offs and landings in Canada.

Danger is greatest to aircraft in the vicinity of airports, where engine failure is most critical, and at Vancouver International Airport hawks and owls proved something of a nuisance. In 1964 and 1965 there were nineteen aircraft strikes from these birds, which had assembled over the runways and grass areas hunting rodents. As the species concerned were—and still are—protected, it was decided to trap them and between 1963 and 1967 more than 500, chiefly short-eared owls, were removed from Vancouver. Efforts were then made to keep the grass too short for rodents, so that these predators were not tempted to hang around the airports looking for food. It is interesting to relate that elsewhere, experiments were conducted to allow grass to grow long on the areas between the runways in an effort to discourage gulls and lapwings from settling. In doing so, perhaps long-eared owls may be encouraged to take up residence with the Jumbo jets!

As increasing food surpluses paved the way towards the industrial revolution and the urban explosion, so the technological revolution has gradually been releasing more and more people from the yoke of full-time work. The leisure boom is already upon us, and it is no exaggeration to say that the impact of millions of people thirsty for adventure, amusement and the sun is proving to be as great upon the countryside as that of the pioneer farmers over the ages wielding their axes and scratching the land with their ploughs.

Although today every man has a right to time off, leisure was once the prerogative of the rich, and one of their favourite forms of amusement was hunting. William the Conqueror did not give a second thought to the removal of his newly acquired subjects from vast tracts of countryside when he decided to improve the stocks of deer, and thus the quality of the chase. Up until the sixteenth century, animals were hunted for sport by stealth, using weapons such as the long bow and crossbow. However, advances in weaponry were soon to change the relationship between the hunter and his quarry. To a person armed with an accurate firearm with a much enhanced range, stealth was perhaps less important and gamebirds were bagged in greater numbers than ever before. Now, sportsmen were capable of shooting their precious game animals out of existence, and so the landed gentry and nobility employed special servants to look after the sporting resources of their estates, and gamekeepers were created. In a very short time, pheasant and partridge rearing systems were devised, and the technique of heather burning was established to boost the populations of red grouse on the moorland.

The pursuit of game has had a very important effect upon the wildlife in Britain as, apart from resulting in the introduction of various exotic species of birds and mammals and their maintenance in large numbers, a vigorous war has been waged upon predatory birds and mammals by generations of keepers over the past two centuries or so. According to traditional game practice, these animals had no place in areas given over to producing wildlife for sport and the pot. The size of the gibbet, and the continual addition of carcases to it, used to be the only means by which the employer could judge the industry of his keepers, and many over the ages doubtless applied themselves enthusiastically to the task of putting on a good show of what they were pleased to call 'vermin'. The policy, although misguided, was quite simple; the more weasels, stoats and sparrow-hawks that could be brought down by the shotgun, or caught in snares, pole or gin traps, the more pheasants or partridges would be stopped in full flight by a well-aimed charge of shot. In those days, to the keepers with a simple down-to-earth view of nature, nothing could have been more obvious.

The effect of game management upon owls, however, is not altogether certain. There is no doubt that tawny owls will take game chicks if the opportunity arises, and they have therefore been classed by keepers as no better than poachers. Old brown owls, however, are not easy targets; they hide by day, and as their hunting method does not make them particularly vulnerable, it seems unlikely that they have suffered as much as the diurnal birds of prey, and the barn owl. The increasing scarcity of the barn owl in the British Isles before the use of organo-chlorine pesticides has already been referred to, and although keepers probably had no cause to blame this species for game losses, the fact does show how prejudiced the gaming fraternity were in their treatment of all predators.

On the Continent, the magnificent eagle owl has suffered tremendously in the 'interests' of good gamekeeping, in fact it is the only species of owl in Europe which has been drastically reduced by man's persecution. For example, bounties were paid by the State for each eagle owl killed, and in France it used to be classed as vermin until well into the 1960s. Although the species is still fairly widespread in parts of Europe—there are between 4,500 and 6,500 pairs left in Sweden, Estonia, Finland, France and both East and West Germany—it is still on the decline. This is most fully documented for Sweden. During the Second World War period there were 455 pairs of eagle

Eagle owl (*Philip Wayre*)

owls, but this number had been reduced to 171 pairs by the mid-1970s.

A further factor in the tragic story of this magnificent owl was its usefulness as a decoy. In France, Italy and Spain live or mounted eagle owls were placed on a tall pole where they attracted birds which would mob the hated intruder. So strong is the mobbing response of birds that they would fail to notice hunters strategically placed with guns. It is not easy to miss at such close range. It is ironical that these rare owls, through being used as lures, have over the ages enticed countless other birds of prey to their doom, and have doubtless helped to clear whole areas of them. Barn and little owls also used to be used in Italy as decoys for larks, which are good to eat; however stylised mechanical lures studded with eyes and flashing wings have now made the real owls redundant, since song birds treat these as they would a real predator. Snowy owls, too, have been shot in Scandinavia, although the decline of the species there might be due to the retreat of the Arctic fauna in some of the fells, rather than to persecution.

In North America, the great horned owl was blamed for taking too many pheasants and grouse. But these birds, and other raptors, also consume great quantities of rodents, and what gamekeepers generally did not understand was, that the extermination of raptors in the 'interests' of game production may allow mice and voles to increase to such an extent that the ground cover may be altered and made unfavourable for pheasants. And since rodents compete with pheasants for food, the removal of predators, particularly those not guilty of taking precious game birds, might affect the season's bag more significantly than the gamekeeper would have predicted. Also, in the case of species that do compete with the shooters, the game animals that are killed by the raptors would not necessarily have been available for sport; the birds may have been taking the unhealthy ones.

It is at least an interesting thought that some owls might actually have profited slightly from the reduction of predators like stoats, weasels, and kestrels. These feed on rodents, among other things, and obviously compete with owls for them. If keepering did result in fewer diurnal vole- and mouse-eating predators, then owls might have had easier hunting by night. But after so many centuries of unremitting persecution, it is a wonder that any birds of prey exist

Tengmalm's owls live mainly in coniferous woodland, using tree holes or old black woodpecker nestholes for breeding (*Hans Reinhard/Bruce Coleman Ltd*)

at all in Europe and North America.

Sometimes gamekeepers have been too quick to lay the blame for their own inefficiency, or the effects of disease or inclement weather on their stock of birds, at the feet of predators. This was the case with the little owl after it had been introduced into England, first in Kent in 1879 and then in Northamptonshire in 1889. In Europe, it had previously been confined to the south, and only stragglers had reached the British Isles, such as one which was taken alive on a boat off Great Yarmouth in 1862. By the turn of the century, the cries of these birds were common in the night chorus in various parts of the English countryside, and the species rapidly spread the length and breadth of the country.

But if bird-watchers were happy at having yet another species to tick off on their tally lists, the gamekeepers, ever on the lookout for pheasant- and partridge-hungry vermin, were not. Their view was that these birds were wholesale destroyers of game chicks, poultry chicks and song birds; reports of these 'savage' owls raiding crops were rife, and one observer blamed a little owl for taking thirty-six chickens whose remains were alleged to have been found in its nest. And the fact that as many as seventy-two were killed around a single poultry farm could not have done anything to reassure farmers. In 1922, Felstead School's Science Society blamed these aliens for decimating the population of small ground-nesting birds like tree pipits. The idea was even put forward that the decline of the barn owl on the Thames marshes was due to competition with its smaller cousin. This notoriety was all the more surprising considering that, as long ago as three centuries before Christ, Aristotle had said that they hunt mice, lizards and beetles, and even today the little owl is prized by gardeners in Italy for its uncommon ability in destroying insects, snails and slugs. In parts of Holland, farmers have even encouraged it as an anti-rodent measure.

In 1935 a decision had to be made as to whether the little owl should be protected by law or classed as 'vermin'. The British Trust for Ornithology set up an inquiry into the food habits of this alien,

The great horned owl inhabits a variety of American habitats from the boreal forests of the Arctic to tropical mangrove swamps (*Stephen J. Krasemann/Bruce Coleman Ltd*)

and the results were collated by Alice Hibbert-Ware. Some 2,460 food pellets and the gizzards of twenty-eight little owls were analysed, together with material taken from seventy-six nests. Some were collected from game-rearing estates, and appeals were made over the radio for any evidence of widespread predation upon pheasants or poultry chicks; none materialised. One and a half years of intensive investigation revealed only two pellets, each with the remains of one game chick. A doubtful one turned up in a gizzard, and evidence of seven consumed poultry chicks was found. The remains of 10,217 earwigs (343 in one pellet), burying and ground beetles, cockchafers and weevils were discovered, and many of these are harmful to horticulture. It is not surprising, then, that in Hungary, Switzerland and Germany, where its utility is beyond doubt, this alien is protected by law. Since the British Trust for Ornithology inquiry was published, few voices have been raised against the little owl, which curiously has been on the decline in much of southern and central England over the last half century, well before toxic chemicals raised their heads, although its range is still extending into northern England and southern Scotland.

During the last decade or two there has been a great arousal of people's interest and concern for wildlife. The destruction of habitats has too often led to a diminished variety of animals and plants, and the very existence of others has been threatened. In those countries where people are generally aware of, and interested in, their wildlife resources, protective legislation has been put on the statute books to give some force to the conservationists. In fact, it is interesting to note that the attitude of different nations to their countryside can be gauged by the organisation of wildfowling, and to the protective measures given to birds of prey in those countries. In a way, these act as a kind of litmus paper to public opinion on nature, the countryside, and its resources.

In Great Britain, the Wildlife and Countryside Act 1981 affords all owls protection, and gives the diminishing but still widespread barn owl and very rare snowy owl special protection even from naturalists. Nest robbers and those convicted of killing members of either of these two species face a £2,000 fine. With so many people now turning to ornithology as part of the leisure boom, the act even safeguards the best interests of the birds; permission is required from the Nature Conservancy Council to set up a hide for photographing these lovely creatures at their nests.

Similar attempts at controlling the ruthless, or thoughtless, nature photographer were made in Sweden. Twenty-six of the country's finest wildlife camera hunters formed themselves into a consortium (*Naturfotografernas Bildförmedling*), which laid down a code of ethics for their profession and operates as a clearing house for their wares. This was partly in reaction to the widespread and indiscriminate use of faked prints by journal editors, involving more often than not stuffed museum specimens. The second reason was the sensible realisation that much 'nest-site' photography is unnecessarily duplicated, and in cases where the location is 'gardened'—that is when inconvenient branches have to be trimmed back—the result is ultimately as lethal to the chicks as if the photographer had pressed the trigger of a 12-bore shotgun every time he, or she, squeezes the camera teat. These Swedish naturalists have, therefore, drawn up a list of those species which they consider to have been adequately covered at their nests, and they accordingly suggest that these should not, for the time being at least, be further harassed by hides and the popping of electronic flashes. The eagle owl is included on this list of VIBs, together with the sea eagle and the osprey.

In Norway, eight out of ten kinds of breeding owl have been protected since 1932, but the snowy owl is only totally safe in the national parks, and the breeding season outside these areas. In 1960, eagle owls were recommended for complete protection in the breeding season. Elsewhere in Europe, owls are also given legal shelter. In Germany this is afforded under the Game Law (*Bundesjagdgesetz*), and similarly in Switzerland, while in Holland the 9,000 or so pairs of owls of all species nesting there do so without undue fear of the gun or pole trap. Belgium and France, however, were always problem countries; the Caen Working Conference on Birds of Prey and Owls in 1964 sowed fertile seeds of conservation in the French government, which later decreed that the eagle owl, together with the osprey, white-tailed and short-toed eagles, should be given total protection. But laws are of little use if they are not enforced, in which case they are generally flouted.

Education is most important, first to persuade people that it is good to have live birds around, thus making sense of legislation, and secondly to ensure that shooters and gamekeepers, who are in a position to kill protected species, are able to distinguish them from other quarry. As part of this education, owls, for example, have been featured on postage stamps. The principality of Monaco proclaimed the barn owl on one of its conservation stamps as being a useful species and, perhaps in recognition of its services as a rodent catcher, Poland portrayed a fine eagle owl on a stamp. Other countries, too, have chosen owls to feature on their stamps, no doubt with valuable resultant publicity for these birds.

As well as protection stamps, the Royal Society for the Protection of Birds in the United Kingdom produced a fine poster, one of their early ones, featuring a barn owl crouched over a rat. 'Wanted, alive!' it proclaimed, in the fashion of a poster seen pinned up in every Hollywood-style sheriff's office. 'Last heard of in nearly every country parish'. 'Occupation, rodent destroyer'. 'Reward for sparing its life—more food for humans'. 'Know your friends'. This particular piece of publicity proved rather too effective at times; many country folk took the opening promulgation too seriously and several turned up at local police stations to deliver live barn owls into the rather baffled long arm of the law. Whether these people were then persuaded to join the Royal Society for the Protection of Birds, the other main object of the poster, is not known, but it has since been withdrawn (see p 157).

Then there is the problem of educating those who shoot for sport, or manage estates for their game. In countries like France, Italy and Malta, there is a strong tradition of shooting virtually anything that moves, with little thought for tomorrow's sport. Fortunately in Great Britain, and also particularly in the United States where there are over eighteen million sport hunters, hunting is reasonably well controlled, and wildlife conservation is taken seriously. But the traditional gamekeepers, a few of whom are still left, have yet to understand that predatory birds and mammals have an amenity value in themselves. They are, admittedly, highly mobile and will tend to concentrate where the hunting is good, and a more than usually abundant supply of bobwhites or pheasants will, of course, attract birds like the horned owls. Nevertheless, good game managers today will not attempt a full-scale extermination policy which, to be effective, would involve killing birds of prey over a very wide area in view of their nomadic way of life. Today, emphasis should be on making the game birds less easy to catch, by providing cover and sheltered feeding spots. No matter how thick on the ground pheasants or bobwhites are, predators are not going to hang around if they are hard to find.

Radio, and lately television, have undoubtedly played their part in the more advanced countries in encouraging a more enlightened attitude towards wildlife, by means of their natural history programmes; and societies like the Royal Society for the Protection of Birds have been campaigning since 1889 on behalf of bird welfare. Furthermore, in the British Isles and in the United States, conservation stories are now becoming widely reported in the mass media, so we can perhaps look forward to still further improvement in people's attitude to wildlife.

It is perhaps a reflection of the troubled nuclear age in which we live that many people are greatly concerned for rare and vanishing forms of wildlife, whose continuing existence is perhaps as tenuous as their own. Organisations like the Worldwide Fund for Nature, the Fauna and Flora Preservation Society, and the International Union for the Conservation of Nature are all fighting to save remnant populations of a depressingly large number of species. However, rarity must be put into perspective; after all, extinction, as well as success, is the thousand-million-year story of evolution, and no species lasts forever. Populations either slowly alter to meet the ever-changing conditions of life, or lose out in competition with other more efficient kinds in the survival game. It is too easy to forget that species have a 'life expectation', and that not every population that disappears today has necessarily vanished at the hand of man.

Nevertheless, there is evidence that the extinction rate of wildlife is running far beyond the natural level, and that this is due to the destructive sides of civilisation discussed earlier in this chapter. For example, James Fisher has looked carefully at the fossil record for the last million or two years and reckons that the life expectation of bird species dropped steadily from 1 ½ million years to 40,000 years, due chiefly to the savage effect of the ice ages—the ice age overkill! Since the seventeenth century, however, the extinction rate has rocketed, and nowadays the species life expectancy is nearer 16,100 years. This means that the majority of the planet's vanished kinds of wild birds have been pushed over the brink by man, the tool-maker, who in this context could have been more aptly named as the undertaker. A scholarly book, *Extinct and Vanishing Birds of the World*, written by James Greenway Jr, brings home the impact of the trappings of civilisation on avian life, and certainly makes for sobering reading—all 520 pages of it. Since the last dodo drew its last breath in 1681 on the island of Mauritius, seventy-eight species and forty-nine sub-species or races of birds have vanished, and can now only be seen as lifeless skins collecting dust in museum cases.

Owls have not escaped the last 300 years unscathed, although when their record is compared with those of parrots, the flightless rails, and the tasty pigeons and ducks, it would seem that they have not come off too badly. Island forms have probably suffered more than their continental relatives because they are peculiarly vulnerable to disturbance. To begin with, their populations are usually numerically small, and so the killing of a few might reduce the species beyond the point of no return. Secondly, islands can be paradises, not only for man but also for birds. Competition from related mainland forms is often lacking, and, free of enemies, the reward for those that reach oceanic atolls may be a life of ease. The birds lose their suspicion and fear and may nest in exposed positions.

Later on, when these islands and their fauna are discovered, if the birds are not exploited for the pot, their 'coup de grâce' may be delivered by the animals following in our footsteps. We are great re-distributors, and wherever we go a host of wild, and not so wild, life tags on behind us. Pigs eat almost anything, and root around destroying ground nests and eggs; sheep and goats are as efficient vegetation croppers as anything, and may destroy plant cover. Rats are by now ubiquitous, and although they may be welcomed by large owls, they play havoc among colonial nesting birds. Mongooses and cats are often world-wide hitch-hikers, and are all too efficient at making meals of confiding birds. So far as predators are concerned, the Cape barn or grass owls have been introduced into the Seychelles and in Hawaii, to the detriment of a number of nesting birds as well as the rats it was hoped that they would control, while the little owl is now a familiar part of New Zealand's avifauna, as well as of our own.

Practically all of the handful of recently extinct owls have been islanders. One and a half centuries after the extinction of the dodo on Mauritius, Commerson's owl (*Otus commersoni*) gave its last hoot. It was a large bird, practically 2ft (60cm) long with prominent ear tufts and legs devoid of feathers. A French naturalist, J. Desjardins, wrote of a certain Dr Dobson shooting one in the wood of Curipipe in 1837; since then nothing has been heard or seen of this fine owl, which is known only by a drawing and a description. Bones of another species, *Tyto sanzieri*, have been found on Mauritius. The neighbouring island of Rodriguez has fared no better, having been used as a kind of chandler's store by early sailors. Unfortunately, the goods did not last long. A fluffy rail, *Aphanapteryx*, survived until 1730, together with a night heron, *Nycticorax megacephalus,* and a parrot, *Necropsittacus rodericanus*; the Rodriguez little owl, *Athene murivora*, was not seen after that fateful year. The solitaire, a relative of the dodo and, at 40lb (18kg), as heavy as a big turkey, hung on until 1791, whereas a fine crested starling, *Fregilupus rodericanus,* survived another forty years. Another related species, the forest spotted owlet, *Athene blewitti*, seems to have disappeared from the dense forest habitat in central India, where it had always been rare. The last one was 'collected' in 1914.

A number of island races have also been lost in the last two centuries. The explorer Humboldt 'collected' thirty Comoro scops owls, *Otus rutilus capnodes,* and may have killed them all, because none has been reported this century. Two West Indian forms of the widespread, through local, burrowing owl disappeared around 1890, shortly after the introduction of the mongoose. As these long-legged owls nest in burrows, they would have been easily caught by such fast mammalian killers. Even on the mainland of North America the status of the Western burrowing owl is giving grounds for worry. These owls depend upon such mammals as prairie dogs for their homes, and so the changing pattern of agriculture practised on the prairies, together with the ceaseless war waged upon rodents, is operating against the interest of these birds. In California, for example, the United States Government has poisoned and sealed mammal burrows, and many broods of burrowing owls must have been destroyed. Shooting, and the prevalence of semi-feral cats, have also contributed towards the decrease. Reserves, and preservation of the coteries upon which they depend for their nest sites, seems to be the only answer to this problem.

New Zealand has lost a magnificent owl. The Antipodes has two indigenous species; the morepork is a widespread Australasian owl, but the larger laughing owl (*Sceloglaux albifacies*)—or the whekau as the Maoris called it—is a New Zealand speciality; or was, because it proved to be particularly sensitive to the changes wrought on 'The Land of the Great White Cloud' by Europeans, so that it is doubtful whether any survive today. Indeed, hardly had the birds come to the attention of the first settlers—when it was plentiful on the Southern Island—than it started to disappear from its haunts. Apparently laughing owls inhabited open country, making their 'lairs' inside the fissures of rocky outcrops. Nesting began in September, the cock apparently taking over from the hen some of the burden of incubation. Worms, beetles, lizards and native rats were hunted on foot because, like so many of New Zealand's native birds, these owls were feeble fliers, making up for this shortfall by possessing rather long but powerful legs.

Specimens, both alive and dead, were dispatched from the colony to London, and several healthy birds were displayed before a meeting of the Zoological Society at Regent's Park on 3 November 1874. Two of these eventually acted as models for the fastidious artist J.G. Keulemans, who illustrated Sir Walter Buller's classic volume *The History of the Birds of New Zealand*. Sadly, Keulemans's fine portrait was as near as most naturalists of his day ever came to seeing these robust-looking owls. By then, they were becoming very rare, perhaps due to the carnage caused by a bevy of alien carnivores. Ferrets and cats were devastating the confiding native species, and the Government had liberated weasels to help to suppress the 'rabbit nuisance'.

Although some optimists suspect that the laughing owl still lingers in remote parts of the southern Alps, the last authentic record is of a dead one discovered at Bluecliffs, South Canterbury, in July 1914 by a Mrs Airini Woodhouse. The bird was duly mounted beneath a glass dome and kept in her house. However, for those who never give up hope, the advice is to take up the accordion because, according to a story recalled by Sir Walter Buller, the owls could be lured into the open by the strains of one of these instruments!

Tyto ostologa.
An extinct barn owl
from the Carribean,
known only from bone
fragments. The size
of a snowy owl.

Seychelles owl

New Zealand laughing owl or whekau

The extinct
burrowing owl
of the West Indies

SOME EXTINCT AND VANISHING OWLS

But other owls have fared better in that far-off land. Early New Zealand colonists, in their attempt to re-create an idyllic British countryside down under, liberated many European species, including both the tawny and little owl. Between 1906 and 1910 several shipments of little owls were released in Otago and, together with skylarks, song thrushes, blackbirds and goldfinches, have become an established part of the Antipodean wildlife. Those homesick settlers were responsible for upsetting the delicate relationships established over millions of years between native animals and plants, and New Zealand is now a hotch-potch of aliens and natives. Many of the latter have profited from the tearing down of the forests, whereas others, like the moas and huias, have suffered irretrievably. There is evidence that even the morepork might be reduced in certain habitats because of competition with the little owl. The former proved to be fairly adaptable, and even spread from the native forests into urban districts, but in the 1930s it began to decrease in the Christchurch city area and at the same time the numbers of the European immigrant increased. Unfortunately there is no shortage of owls in peril.

In 1988, the International Council for Bird Protection published a checklist of threatened species called 'Birds to Watch'. It made solemn reading, drawing attention to 1,029 kinds—equivalent to one species in nine—potentially heading for extinction. The figure represents an astonishing leap since the previous survey in 1978 when ICBP's Red Data Book documented 290 endangered bird species. The burgeoning tally of crippled bird populations is a sad reflection on the world's deteriorating habitats. Owls are well represented, and several may well be beyond rescuing. Most come from the tropics. The Madagascar red owl (*Tyto soumagnei*) from the rain forests in the central part of the island has only been observed once since 1934, and that was in 1973. Both the unique lemurs and this owl are threatened by the wholesale destruction of the forest sanctuaries. The related Taliabu owl (*Tyto nigrobrunnea*) is restricted to Taliabu in the Sula Islands and known only from a single carcase collected in 1938! Likewise the existence of the Itombwe owl (*Phodilus prigoginei*) from Zaire is based upon only one specimen, but a bay owl almost certainly of this species was present on a tea plantation in Burundi during the 1970s.

White-faced scops owl, *Otus lencotis* (*John Markham*)

The populations of no less than nine kinds of scops owl are in a parlous state. Island faunas are especially fragile and several very rare scops owls languish on island sites, such as the Comoros, Java and Mindoro (in the Phillipines). The Seychelles owl (*Otus insularis*) is confined to Mahé, the principal island of the group. In the tradition of Victorian ornithology, an owl in the bag used to be worth more than a well written description. Accordingly, a certain Michael Nicoll, in March 1906, heard one hooting and tried to secure it—without success. Although shortly afterwards the species was declared extinct, it miraculously reappeared in 1959. It is now thought that there may be about 80 pairs in the upland forests of Mahé where, however, a certain amount of logging is inevitable.

One eagle owl (*Bubo vosseleri*) from the Usambara Mountains in north-east Tanzania is at risk from the implacable march of forest clearance. Both the rufous fishing owl (*Scotopelia ussheri*) and Blakiston's fish owl (*Ketupa blakistoni*) are mentioned. The former inhabits mangrove swamps and forests bordering rivers and lakes in West Africa, whereas the latter species ranges sparsely across the Soviet Far East, northern China, and Hokkaido, Japan. There may be 300–400 pairs left in the USSR but a survey in 1984 located only about 50 Japanese birds. North America boasts one rare owl, the spotted (*Strix occidentalis*) from the mature woodlands of the west. Commercial logging from south-west Canada through to central Mexico is the most important threat. Not only are the owl's favoured surroundings destroyed, but the increased competition from more robust barred owls, and predation by great-horned owls in areas of secondary growth, are likewise harmful. Conservationists in the States have recently moved against loggers in a bid to save the owls—and won. The Puerto Rican short-eared and Virgin Island screech owls also survive in very low numbers, but these are simply rare races of more widespread continental forms.

On a more hopeful note, we are now, with some animals at least, almost in the position of reversing the natural extinction process by bringing small populations into zoos or wildlife parks and encouraging them to breed. Had it not been for the timely action of the eleventh Duke of Bedford in bringing together at Woburn Park practically all of the surviving Père David's deer, these fine Chinese animals would probably by now have been lost to the world. A significant proportion of the total population of the Arabian oryx is also being kept at Phoenix Zoo, Arizona, as an insurance policy against the extinction of these mammals in the wild. It may even one day be possible to build up such a surplus stock of rare species as to make it feasible to reintroduce populations into their native habitats where they once flourished. Owls, unlike hawks, seem to pose no special problems in captivity and, providing they are given reasonable space, food, nest sites and privacy, will breed quite well behind wire netting. Reference has already been made to the breeding success of elf owls in Washington Zoo (see p63). The 1970 edition of the *International Zoo Yearbook*, published by the Zoological Society of London, contained a supplement on Birds of Prey in Captivity, and there reference was made to the successful breeding of such species as spectacled, snowy, woodfords, Javan fishing, barn, little, and a variety of eagle owls. Although nobody has yet attempted to breed any of the really rare owls with a view to building up stocks in zoos, there has been one well-thought-out scheme to aid conservation of eagle owls in both Sweden and Germany and its success may well encourage others to try similar schemes with the really endangered species.

From the sixteenth to the eighteenth centuries, eagle owls were reasonably common throughout the whole of Sweden, but by the end of the last century there was a sudden decrease, and by 1925 the species had disappeared from the southern parts of the country. According to Dr Viking Olsson, who had been studying them, there were about 455 breeding pairs between 1943 and 1948, but after that the situation became critical and by 1965 the total Swedish population was closer to 175 pairs. In the 1950s, a scheme was launched to introduce eagle owls into the Kilsbergen mountain range, which was considered to be an excellent habitat for these birds and which had lost its last breeding pair in 1937. With the help of the Nordiska Museum and Skansen in Stockholm, a re-establishment operation was drawn up. Birds were obtained from zoos, and particularly from the Norfolk Wildlife Park in Great Britain which, under the ownership of Philip Wayre (chairman of the Conservation Committee of the British Federation of Zoological Gardens) has always had an enlightened policy of animal breeding. Philip Wayre's success with eagle owls was nothing short of staggering, and up to 1969 no less than eighteen eagle owls were exported from this park to Sweden. However, the success of the Swedish experiment depended upon the full co-operation of the local people, who regarded the eagle owl with mixed feelings. In order to win them over, 'Eagle Owl' meetings or 'teach-ins' were organised on Saturday evenings in the villages around the introduction area and, lured by music and light refreshments, those who attended were treated to a talk which outlined the aims of the scheme and hoped to allay the fears and prejudices of the people who, after all, had to live with the owls. Another similar scheme was established in the Eifel area, north-west Germany, by the Deutscher Naturschutzring. In all, about 200 owls were released in Germany, 13 being provided by Philip Wayre, and the species is now well established in that area.

The manner of the introduction is just as important as winning over anyone who is likely to place these owls squarely in their gun-sights. Birds which have spent their lives in captivity are not best

Eagle owl family

equipped to survive in the wild. Food has always been available to them with the minimum of effort, and a tame zoo owl is just as likely to sit around and starve to death in its new unrestricted world. It was, therefore, decided that a large aviary should be built in the proper habitat and zoo-bred pairs of eagle owls housed inside them. As these birds settle down well in captivity and rear families with little trouble, it was assumed correctly that they would do the same in their forest cages in Kilsbergen. The offspring of these original pairs would then be allowed to gain the freedom of the woods in their own time. In 1956, the first pair produced two owlets and these were released in the October of their first year. Gradually their excursions into the forest took them farther afield, although they returned 'home' each day to be fed. Making food available during the first few months is an important part of the plan because it probably gives breathing space to the owlets, which need time to practise their hunting techniques. As they gain proficiency the home visits become more irregular and then cease altogether.

Release schemes are not always an unqualified success as those involving barn owls in Great Britain reveal. Injured owls, very often road victims, have good breeding potential. When given unlimited supplies of food, captive pairs produce brood after brood of owlets; sixteen a year is not unusual. From such aviary-bred sources, between 1,500 and 2,000 barn owls are released back into the countryside by as many as 400 operators. However, as an exercise to supplement Britain's ailing barn owl population, the results are rather mixed. As many as three out of four birds die during their first year—a normal level of mortality for this species, so for every pair that manages to establish itself, four or five vanish. A well monitored programme carried out by the Hawk Trust in Buckinghamshire in which 22 pairs were released resulted in only 3 pairs of owls attempting to nest. The problem is that many re-introduction schemes cover areas where barn owls may already be surviving, at critically low levels and held in check by sub-standard environments. In these places, therefore, there is literally no room for more owls. The best results tend to be where individuals are liberated in April or May into territories of wild unmated owls.

In 1987, Colin Shawyer formulated a conservation strategy for this species. He pointed out that the long-term prospects for this and other species could only improve if the habitat and thus food supply were reinstated. The barn owl in particular needs plentiful rough grassland, with good corridors along the edges of woodlands, fields and river courses so that, if necessary, it can move between farms and estates in its quest for rodents. The plan also stressed the need for nest sites such as suitable outbuildings, hollow trees and, if necessary, the use of artificial owl nest boxes. If carried out, Shawyer's plan will bring back the once-familiar sight of these ghostly white owls floating along the hedgerows, searching for their evening meals.

Apart from the very rare ones, owls are luckily fairly competent at looking after themselves—they are superbly camouflaged and feed mostly at night and so out of sight. Accordingly many species, like tawny and screech owls, are in a reasonably healthy state. People are also mostly on their side and this happy fact is enshrined in legislation designed to protect wildlife on both sides of the Atlantic. In Europe virtually all owls are protected by the laws of the land—East Germany is apparently an exception, giving protection only to eagle and pigmy owls. However, policing the law is another problem, and in Italy and Malta many owls still fall victim to trigger-happy hunters. And even in the United Kingdom where there is a long tradition of caring for birds, illegal pole traps still kill raptorous species, and avaricious egg thieves keep up pressure on rare species. So far, there is only one reserve in Europe designated for birds of prey and that is at Sabed, near the town of Tirgu Mures in Romania; scops, little and tawny owls enjoy the safety of the place.

Meanwhile, what can we do to ensure a good and vigorous population of our other native owls? Providing their habitats are preserved and there is the maximum of goodwill from people, the owls should be able to look after themselves. Their natural surroundings will supply them with food and nest sites—both conditions for survival—though in some cases nest sites might be in very short supply, particularly in great areas of tidy forestry plantations where all the trees are kept healthy and cut down in their prime for timber. Efforts should, therefore, be made to preserve old hollow trees which may be useless commercially but which provide roost and nest sites for owls.

So much for our brief survey of living owls and mankind. The relationship has had a chequered career, but on the whole one must

WANTED – ALIVE!

THE BARN - OWL

Last heard of in nearly every country parish. Occupation, rodent destroyer. Reward for sparing its life—more food for humans! Protected by law! Know your friends, preserve the countryside and its birds, and support the ROYAL SOCIETY FOR THE

PROTECTION OF BIRDS

This early RSPB poster had the unfortunate effect of encouraging well-meaning helpers to flood police stations with live owls.

conclude that owls have not fared too harshly. Of the future, we can only hope that, with the increasing awareness of wildlife and the countryside, man will look favourably upon the birds which seem to emulate him in so many ways, and that the owls will prosper bountifully in all places. But should the forecast be bleak and the land one day be covered entirely with concrete and tarmac, and the skies filled with only house sparrows, starlings, feral pigeons and herring gulls, we might still hazard a guess that the hoots of that opportunist, the tawny, will somewhere echo across the night landscape. Let us hope there is better promise for the future and that the naked ape will show something of the wisdom he has so readily attributed to owls.

5 *Owls of all Shapes and Sizes*

The story of owls starts nearly sixty million years ago when the world was a very different kind of place. An enormous time span of seventy or more million years of reptilian domination had come to an end and warm-blooded, furry mammals were proving to be promising upstarts. Many of these were magnificent beasts that failed to pass the test of time; rhino-sized amblypods with bizarre knobs and horns sprouting from their skulls were probably familiar to the first North American owls. Other giants like titanotheres, and an 18ft (5.4m) high rhinoceros, *Baluchitherium*, also tramped the warm plains in those far-off days. A visitor from the twentieth century AD would have looked in vain for familiar shapes and forms. Elephants and cats had not evolved, and man was not even a twinkle in the eyes of lemur-like primates. The horses that we know so well today were still in their prototype stage; they were the size of terriers and had four toes on each leg planted firmly on the ground. The landscape of conifers, cycads, palms and deciduous trees was probably not gilded by any gay arrays of flowers; magnolias had by then made an entrance but orchids, now so coveted and admired, were still millions of years off.

Birds had then been around for eighty million years or so, and had come a long way from the whip-tailed, toothed *Archaeopteryx*, which doubtless had fluttered out of the way of 90ft (27m) long dinosaurs like *Diplodicus*, blundering and browsing their way through lagoonside vegetation. The only feature which distinguished those early birds from small bipedal reptiles was their feathers. Those unique evolutionary innovations were both warm and excellent camouflage and, as it turned out, just right to serve as aerofoils, being both light and of large surface area. With time, the reptilian skeleton changed into a lightweight airframe; the tail shortened to the familiar 'parson's nose' (or uropygium), the teeth became redundant and were lost, and the bones of wrist and hand evolved into a stronger layout giving more rigid support to the wing; the brain also became modified to deal with the balancing skills necessary for flight. Sixty million years ago, at the beginning of the Eocene period (geologists have divided up the enormous time spans into periods, all of which have names), birds were modern in appearance. Even so, one suspects that the dawn chorus would have been less pleasing to our ears because some of the world's best choristers, the thrushes, had not yet come upon the scene.

But even if the ears of Eocene creatures were assaulted by tuneless avian croaks and squawks, their eyes were treated to some gigantuan monster birds like *Diatryma*. This was a period when mammals and birds were competing on equal terms for the kingdom gradually being vacated by the scaly dinosaurs and their kin. *Diatrymae* were perhaps the birds' answer to the lion or leopard, and were voracious flesh-eating rails standing 7ft (2m) high and too heavy to fly. Later on they were to be ousted from their position by the big cats. There were plenty of giant vegetarians, too, equivalent perhaps to antelope or cattle. Ostrich-like elephant birds were strutting around by the late Eocene period, and at least one, called *Aepyornis maximus*, stood 8-10ft (2.4-3m) high and must have weighed nearly 1,000lb (450kg)—perhaps the largest bird ever.

Birds, however, only managed to dominate both the skies and the ground for any length of time in places where they were sheltered from the competitive 'mammals. But sheltered areas give false security on a geological time-scale, where a million years counts for nothing, and such places have turned out to be fools' paradises. In Madagascar, the elephant birds clung on until man, the explorer and hunter, set foot there, and then their days were really numbered. New Zealand likewise was a bird's paradise before the Maoris, and later on the Europeans, colonised the islands. In that mammal-free continent (apart from bats), birds like moas took over the role of grazing beasts. A similar story could be repeated for many oceanic islands, too.

The first owl to appear in the fossil record was called *Protostrix mimica*, and its remains were uncovered in the south side of Ten Mile Creek, twelve miles north-west of Worland, in Wyoming. The bones of this owl had lain undisturbed and petrified for nearly sixty million years; even so long ago owls were recognisably owls. Like modern ones, *Protostrix* probably had a well-developed sense of hearing, facial discs, and good night vision. The layout of the toes, two in front and two behind, might also have been similar to that of present-day species and nicely arranged to take a firm grip on wriggling prey. Although all four species of *Protostrix* so far discovered have come to light in North America, the typical owls placed in the family *Strigidae*, and the barn and Asian bay owls separated from the others by anatomical features and given a family—*Tytonidae*—all to themselves, probably originated in what is now Eurasia. France has yielded the earliest fossils of these 'modern' families, and from the findings it seems that the hoots of *Bubos* and *Asios* (eagle and 'eared' owls respectively) could have been heard perhaps thirty-six million years ago in the Oligocene period. The barn owls are, by comparison, a young family and their bones began to turn up in rocks and deposits estimated to be late Miocene in origin, about twelve million years old. At this time our ancestors were still just another type of ape, whereas horses had all but come to look like smaller versions of modern steeds.

Owls did not just suddenly appear fortuitously at the beginning of the Eocene period. The conditions at the time must have favoured the survival of night-operating predatory birds. In retrospect, it seems as though nature always tends to exploit all possible opportunities as and when they arise. As new animals evolve, then others preying upon them also develop.

Each animal in a population differs slightly from all others in its genetical make-up, and some individuals may take advantage of new situations or develop new modes of behaviour. The stakes are high; although success means leaving many surviving offspring to carry the hereditary blueprint for survival, failure means, at the least, personal extinction, or at the worst, species extinction. This natural variation found within animal populations is the raw material of evolution and the preferential survival of some of these is called natural selection; this is the means by which species change and new groups evolve from pre-existing ones to proliferate actively—as the owls did sixty million years ago.

The history of owls cannot be considered in complete isolation, and to find out what encouraged the survival and evolution of these birds we must turn to their food supply. Then, as now, rodents probably provided the early owls with their staple diet, but the key to the sudden expansion of rodents and other animals since the Eocene was held by flowering plants, or Angiosperms. Over this period these became the dominant form of vegetation, and their success was due in no small way to a kind of working partnership struck up between them and certain animals. Flowers advertised and provided food for insects, bats and birds in return for the service of pollination; juicy fruits enticed all manner of animals to collect and eat them, and to aid dispersal of the resilient seeds they concealed. As a means to reproduction and dispersal, it was an evolutionary hit and the success of both Angiosperms and their pollinators was assured. The seeds also provided vast supplies of food which both mammals and birds were able to exploit.

The ramifications in so far as birds were concerned, were tremendous; a great many birds feed either directly upon hard seeds (for example, the finches, parrots, weavers and nut-crackers), fruits (such as the pigeons and toucans), or upon insects whose livelihood depends upon flowers (bee-eaters, warblers, and so on). Among the mammals, the rodents have doubtless profited as much from the spread and dominance of Angiosperms and their nourishing seeds as any other group. Indeed the influence has probably been two-way; the 'over-

Owns in some areas of America take over, as night falls, from the daytime hunters

Sparrow hawk

Cooper's hawk

Red-tailed hawk

Marsh hawk

Red-shouldered hawk

Screech owl

Great-horned owl

Short-eared owl

Barred owl

Long-eared owl carrying a young rat (*Eric Hosking*)

production' of fruit might have been due to the excessive toll taken by both birds and rodents, operating on the principle that a few may be overlooked, although the spread of many plants must be aided by the hoarding habit of these animals and their occasional 'forgetfulness'.

So far as rodents are concerned, the last sixty million years have been a period of unbounded evolutionary fertility. Their food supply has increased bountifully and probably allowed them to produce more frequent and larger litters than before, as well as stimulating active speciation. Every habitat all over the world, barring Australia, New Zealand, Antarctica and oceanic islands, had its complement of scurrying, wide-eyed, gnawing little mammals. They have invaded everywhere from tundras to tropical rain forests; they have successfully adapted to deserts on the one hand and to swamps on the other. Some spend their lives scampering around the canopies of trees, whereas others burrow beneath the surface. There are grain crunchers, browsers and grazers, seed-eaters, nut-crackers, omnivores and even insectivores; the smallest would sit comfortably on a penny, whereas the largest now living, the South American capybara, would need an armchair, being the size of a small pig. Three thousand species are known today, as many as all other mammals put together; in terms of total weight or biomass they would probably tip the scales on every other group, including the whales.

The flowering of the rodent family was gathering momentum during the Oligocene and Miocene periods, between thirty-six and twelve million years ago, and it must now come as no surprise that this was the period when modern birds of prey were also in a state of active evolution. The voles, hamsters, beavers, and the North American gophers, all date from the Oligocene period; the Miocene saw the first squirrels leaping through the trees and bounding over the ground, whereas the cavies, rats and mice were relatively late in coming into the picture. They made their entrance almost with the appearance of the first barn owls—perhaps the most skilled hunters by virtue of hearing that the owl family has ever produced. At the end of the Miocene and early Pliocene periods, about twelve million years ago, the rodents were probably reaching their apogee of success.

In a manner of speaking there was, and still is, a tremendous rodent 'cake' for the taking, and birds were not tardy in adapting to this new and expanding source of food. However, the spoils became divided chiefly between two entirely unrelated families, the owls, and the hawks (Falconiformes), which includes 266 species of hawks, falcons, buzzards and eagles. The hawks and owls really play very similar roles in nature. They have an overall similarity to each other because both have independently developed the 'tools' of their trade as killers—remarkably keen eyesight, strong grasping talons, curved beaks and powerful flight muscles. Nevertheless, there are fundamental differences of anatomy and behaviour between the two groups. Owls have no crop, and often bolt their small mammal food whole, although the skulls of their prey may first of all be crushed by the bill; the head may sometimes be discarded. Bird prey, however, is usually prepared by plucking the wing or tail feathers, and then eaten piecemeal. Hawks, more often than not, tear up their food, and in common with owls, birds taken as prey are usually plucked first. In owls, the outer toes (fourth) can be rotated to join the hind toe and oppose the other two forward-pointing ones. The osprey, a fish-eating raptor, also has this ability, although the other diurnal birds of prey have only one opposable hind toe. Owls do, however, share with the falcons (*Falco* species) a general tendency not to build nests, and this has also been used as evidence of the possible close relationship between them.

These two groups of predatory birds have pursued independent lines of development which complement each other inasmuch as the Falconiformes have specialised as daytime hunters, depending upon sight and speed to surprise their prey, while the owls, using hearing to supplement vision, have taken over their role at night and feed on nocturnal and crepuscular creatures. Sometimes owls and hawks even replace each other, species by species, in an incredibly neat way, so that in any given habitat predatory birds cover the ground throughout the whole of every twenty-four hours. The Craigheads, to whom reference has already been made (see p96), found that short-eared owls were the nocturnal equivalents of hen harriers (or marsh hawks, as the Americans prefer to call this species), both in their hunting methods and prey. Two diurnal species replaced the horned owl; the fast-flying bird-catcher, Cooper's hawk, and the chiefly rodent-killing red-tailed hawk (a kind of buzzard). Where they overlapped, the red-shouldered hawk (a species of buzzard) was similar in its requirements to the barred owl; the rough-legged hawk (or buzzard) and sparrowhawk (an 8½in/21.5cm falcon) to the barn and screech owls respectively. The Craigheads concluded that the outstanding feature of the dovetailing was that a pattern of hunting was formed which largely eliminated direct competition. This was all the more striking because most of the birds were feeding largely upon the same food supply. It was a population of predators composed of different species, each adapted to hunt either a different habitat or the same habitat in a different manner or at a different time.

Owls and other predatory animals must also have had an influence on the evolution of their prey. The reason why night-living animals are camouflaged and wary is because the survival of individuals is seriously hampered if their colour deviates from the hue and pattern best adapted to allow them to melt into their surroundings. To take an extreme example, one suspects that an albino wood or white-footed mouse would be spotted more quickly by the searching eyes of predators. Similarly, an individual that was not constantly alert to movements or sounds indicating the presence of danger would end up in the talons of a hunting owl before its more wary neighbours. Selective mortality of this kind operates as a kind of 'learning process', and the lesson is that with owls at large, darkness does not mean safety for night creatures. In this way the species adapt, and both the behaviour and structure of populations at any time are a result of the selective forces, so that they are kept on their toes, remaining fully alert. Deviants do not survive as well as normal specimens unless they have particular features that may be at a premium and so enhance their owner's survival. In this process owls obviously play a key role.

Owls have, as it were, carved out for themselves a place in the bird world as specialist nocturnal hunters, and their world-wide avian monopoly on the night scene as predators of small animals testifies to their success in this role. However, as a family they have not stood still. Over the last sixty millions years they have undergone what is called an *adaptive radiation*. This term describes the tendency for new animal types to explore all possible avenues of opportunity through natural selection. For example, the first mammals to scurry around this planet were probably rather like shrews and yet, over millions and millions of generations, mammals gradually branched out and took to the water and the air, leaped through the trees and dug their way into the soil; they became almost everything from plankton sievers to carnivores. From the original basic type, mammals of a multitude of different shapes and sizes developed, fitted for as many different occupations. Similarly, birds as a whole have branched out in a big way since those distant days of *Archaeopteryx*, as a cursory glance through the pages of a bird book will suggest. After all, a tiny hummingbird and an ostrich share similar ancestors, yet millions of years of natural selection have fitted out these two birds for very different roles. Adaptive radiation takes place even within families, allowing different species to survive best in certain surroundings and to live off a particular type of food.

A brief survey of the 133 kinds of surviving owls shows that they have undergone an interesting degree of adaptive radiation. As a family, the world is literally their playground (apart from Antarctica), and practically every kind of habitat from the Arctic to the Antipodes, embracing frigid tundra to tropical rain forests, has its quota of these birds. Their habit of sleeping away the day has helped them to penetrate even hot deserts, where certain species like eagle owls emerge from their cool daytime retreats in tree, cactus and cave to hoot and hunt beneath the stars.

Size alone gives some idea of the range of owl occupations, since the bigger the bird the larger the animals upon which it can prey; on this score alone, individual food preferences mean that owls of different kinds, such as the pigmy and eagle owls, can probably co-exist without unduly competing with each other. Even so, there may be a certain degree of overlap, although each species may have its own special hunting technique that helps to avoid competition—individuals may even become specialists, like the eagle owl whose pellets contained almost nothing but the remains of frogs. Nevertheless, size is a fairly good indication of the 'size' of prey. There is a tremendous range of sizes among the more widespread genera of owls. Every continent in the world has its giant variety; apart from the snowy owl, at home in the northerly latitudes, there are the twelve magnificent *Bubos* (eagle and horned), which can tackle prey as large as fawns and rabbits, and rule almost everywhere. And in Australia the long-tailed *Ninox* hawk owls have produced a 20in

Oriental eagle owl, *Bubo sumatrana*

(50cm) bird of *Bubo* size which feeds on largish mammals like rabbits, 'possums and phalangers in the bush country. The fishing owls, too, are large and powerful, and the sienna coloured Pel's of Africa stands 2ft (60cm) high.

There was once even an oversized representative of the barn owls, the *Tytonidae*, but this one is now, alas, extinct. *Tyto ostologa*, as it has been named, used to live in the Caribbean and is known only from bone fragments excavated from bat guano in a cave to the north-west of the Republic of Haiti. These owls probably grew larger than the great horned, and must have been an impressive sight as they quartered the terrain for their prey. Their food probably consisted of very large rodents, remains of which were found alongside those of the owls, which probably had either taken them back to the caves to devour at leisure, or else had regurgitated the remains in pellets. Whether pre-Columbian settlers had anything to do with the disappearance of this species is not too certain; *Tyto ostologa* might have been a casualty in one of the great Ice Age overkills caused by the rapid succession of glacial advances and retreats. What is certain is that the oversized rodents have vanished and this giant barn owl flies no more. Of the eight kinds of barn owl still living, the largest is the masked owl from the Australasian forests, which measures up to 20in (50cm).

At the other end of the scale, the smallest owl in the world is the Least pigmy owl *Glaucidium minutissimum* of Mexico and the Amazon valley, which measures only 4½–5in (11–12cm). Most other members of the genus *Glaucidium* are around the 6in (15cm) mark; in the Himalayas, the cuckoo owlet reaches 10in (25cm). For their size they are voracious little killers with relatively enormous feet and talons for killing mammals almost as large as themselves. Like *Bubo*, the pigmy owls are found in all continents except the Antipodes and Australia.

On the whole, the scops and screech owls (*Otus*) are slightly larger than the pigmy owls, and the thirty eared species are spread across the world, though again the chain is broken by Australia and the south-west Pacific islands. The largest is 12in (30cm) (the giant scops owl, *Otus gurneyi*, from the Philippines), and they seem to have exploited every habitat open to them in the temperate and tropical zones. In North America, the screech owls of the desert regions are

Little owl with female ghost swift moth in beak (*Stephen Dalton*)

smaller than their relatives living at high altitudes or latitudes, because heat loss is facilitated by surface area of the body and increases proportionally with decrease in size.

In this smallish-sized group are the little owls (*Athena*), and the burrowing owl (*Speotyto*). Both of these species tend to hunt on foot and have relatively long legs for walking. Those of the burrowing owl are especially long and bare. No larger are four kinds of *Aegolius* (boreal, unspotted saw-whet, saw-whet and buff-fronted owls). These are like miniature versions of the eleven species of *Strix* wood owls, which includes the tawny, barred and their kin; this genus has produced one big species, the 24–30in (60–75cm) great gray owl— with rather a small body—although the majority of the others are 12–20in (30–50cm) in length. Apart from the tawny, the *Strix* owls have not penetrated Africa, where they are replaced by the wood owl, *Ciccaba wodfordii*. Other *Ciccaba* owls are found in tropical South America, where they no doubt compete with the three odd-looking spectacled species (*Pulsatrix*) which prefer to be near to water in their jungle environment. Within this intermediate-size group must be included six species of eared owls belonging to the genus *Asio*. Four kinds of long-eared owl range from South America to Africa and Madagascar. These show a preference for wooded areas and are, on the whole, strictly nocturnal; the African marsh owl likewise prefers hunting by night although its close relative, the short-eared owl of the northern steppes and pastures, is more diurnal.

Clearly, the range of prey taken by nocturnal owls varies as much as the difference in size between the diminutive 4½in (11cm) long Least pigmy owl to the 2½ft (75cm) giants. Although rodents may well form the staple diet of even the small species, the spectrum of items no doubt differs from one size group to another, and within one group from place to place. Other small mammals, amphibians, reptiles and a whole range of invertebrates from earthworms to insects, are probably taken. The oriental hawk owl (*Ninox scutulata*) has even been recorded as stalking crabs on the coastal mudflats of Burma. As a broad generalisation it could be said that owls are opportunists and take whatever is available. At the same time, however, the smaller prey items can probably be most efficiently sought after, and lived upon, by the small owls, and the selective pressures for maintaining a population of small species has presum-

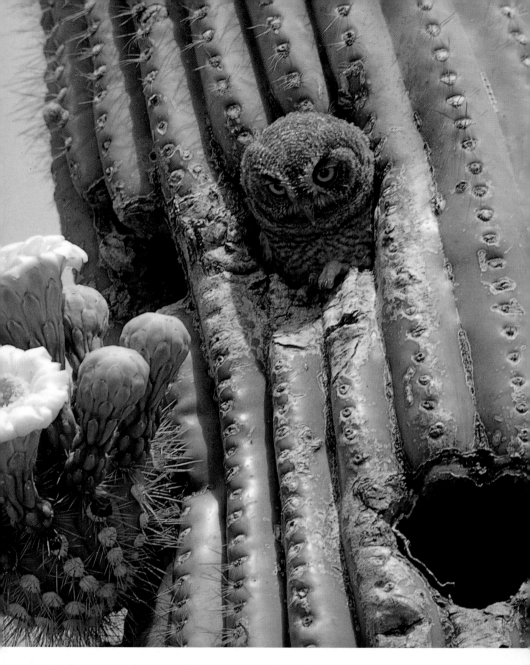

In the cactus deserts of Arizona screech owls excavate nestholes in the giant saguaro (*Jen & Des Bartlett/Bruce Coleman Ltd*)

ably been brought about also by the vast hordes of insects that emerge at sundown. Insects, however, no less then rodents, require specialist hunters, even more so perhaps because they vary so much in size and behaviour. For example, a ciccada, a type of sap-sucking bug, may be crawling up a plant stem in search of a soft spot in which to plunge its sucking proboscis, rustling a leaf or two on the way; it may be singing, or it may be flying swiftly on crackling wings over the treetops in the warm, scented night air. A hungry, crawling ciccada clearly presents quite different problems of detection and interception than does one of these insects on the wing.

Owls are rarely capable of taking all their food on the wing at night. As the owls and hawks have neatly divided up the day, the owls have tended to concentrate on two particular types of night-hunting methods. Many, like the tawny, wait, watch, listen and, after a short sure glide, pounce. Others, like the barn and short-eared owls, tend to patrol on silent wings a few feet above the ground. In both cases hearing is used to supplement vision. The owls which can take a high proportion of insect food, like the elf, pigmy, scops, screech and little owls, do so using typical owl-hunting techniques. Crickets, cicadas, beetles, moths and a host of other types are taken from the ground or foliage. Active hawking has been recorded for some species, however, including the New Guinea hawk owl (*Uroglaux*), the *Ninox* owls and the European scops owl. Even the Akun eagle owl of tropical Africa is reputed to catch cockroaches and other insects on the wing. This insectivorous *Bubo* has a comparatively weak bill and feet for an eagle owl. Nevertheless, owls in general are not built for speed, and for that matter are not the only animals abroad over the moonlit land. Competition both from bats and a group of birds called nightjars may have prevented the owls from evolving insect-chasing techniques, because both these groups were already operating on the wing as night interceptors, and very successfully at that—the job had already been taken!

Bats, incidentally, are the only mammals which have made the technical break-through into flight, and although some are nectar- and fruit-eaters, the majority of the eight hundred species so far

Big ear tufts and orange eyes are the hallmark of the largest European owl, the eagle owl (*W.S. Paton/Aquila Photographics*)

discovered are insectivores. Following small, erratic flying insects at night would probably require vision of unrealistic sensitivity but the bat has perfected an operational technique that helped to solve this problem involving a system of high-frequency sonar location. The sophistication of this method, whereby echoes of the bat's own ultrasonic calls rebounding from the prey give all the clues necessary for interception, is all but beyond our comprehension and has enabled bats to hold a unique position in the night sky all over the world. One species, however, would seem to compete with owls on their own terms; the false vampire, *Vampyrum*, the largest in the New World with a wing span of 30in (75cm), often catches mice. It seems that *Vampyrum* might patrol the South American forests like a barn owl, and be guided to its prey by their rustlings and squeaks.

Bats themselves must be nutritious as food for predators, and they have been dodging and weaving for insects on flickering skin wings certainly since the days of *Protostrix*, but again owls have not been able to develop their own specialised bat interceptor. Although the smaller Australasian hawk owls (*Ninox sp.*) will catch bats, they could not be considered specialists at the job. The diurnal birds of prey, however, have evolved two species which habitually catch these flying mammals. In the New World, the bat falcon (*Falco rufigularis*), like several other falcons, tends to be crepuscular and catches bats and swifts in the mouths of their caves. The most nocturnal member of the Falconiformes, however, is the bat kite (or hawk), *Machaerhampus alcinus*, and in the Old World its range stretches from New Guinea, Borneo and Sumatra to South Africa. It hunts bats, swallows and swifts at twilight and may even fly by the light of the moon. Although its bill is comparatively weak, it has a very wide gape and, like owls, swallows its prey whole. Presumably the basic hunting method of hawks as interceptors allowed them to follow bats into the evening and night, and to prey upon them.

One of the few birds to employ echo-location as a means of navigation is the South American oilbird, *Steatornis caripensis*. This strange bird feeds on palm seeds and nests deep inside cool caves, where it uses its sonar to full advantage. Oilbirds belong to a fascinating group called the Caprimulgiformes, an assembly of ninety-one species which includes the Australasian frogmoths, owlet-

Oilbird on its nesting ledge surrounded by the regurgitated seeds of the fruits on which it feeds at night

nightjars, South American potoos and the more cosmopolitan nightjars. These are all crepuscular and nocturnal in their habits, and depend chiefly upon insects for food. They are also the owl's nearest relatives, though this is not to say that owls evolved from nightjar-like types or vice versa, because it is quite clear that both are at the present time highly modified for their own particular modes of life. Since taxonomists agree that they are close together on the avian family tree, it seems likely that both owls and nightjars share their descent from a common ancestor, perhaps not more than a hundred million years ago. In any case it is interesting that both owl and nightjar lines took to a nocturnal way of life, one tending to specialise in taking chiefly vertebrate prey and the other in flying insects.

Best known of the Caprimulgiformes are the sixty-nine kinds of nightjars (or night hawks), goat-suckers and whip-poor-wills; all are long-winged, long-tailed birds with relatively big eyes obviously capable of extracting enough detail from the twilight and night to allow them to pursue moths, flying cockchafers and so on. But perhaps their most distinctive feature is their enormous mouth, or gape, fringed with rictal bristles that prevent insects from escaping sideways at the last moment before disappearing down the gullet! In a sense, these birds are just like flying insect-traps, or aerial plankton-sievers, and it is possible that part of their food supply is obtained

Least Pygmy 5"   Saw-whet 7½"   Bay 10"   Hawk 15"

Snowy 24"   Spectacled 19"   Long-ea

Milky Eagle 23"

Eagle 30"

4"

Scops 7"

Elf 5¼"

Maximum lengths are given

by literally straining the air as they fly through clouds of dancing
gnats or swarms of other insects. These are the birds which ecologically take over from the swifts, swallows, bee-eaters, and perhaps
even the crepuscular hunting falcons (like hobbies and eleanoras
falcons) by night. So, as owls sit and wait with eyes and ears tuned
to rustles and squeaks on the ground, the nightjars whisper by on
long, pointed wings, only their bill snaps punctuating the silence.

Not all Caprimulgiformes are insect chasers. In Australasia, north-
wards to Malaya, live twelve peculiar kinds of goat-suckers called
frogmouths. Unlike others of their kin, they hunt owl-fashion by
pouncing on to millipedes, scorpions and the like. The 19in (48cm)
long tawny frogmouth of Australia, with a hooked bill and a gape
of staggering proportions, will even take mice, and so ecologically
could be considered a sort of nightjar-owl, a kind of parallel
development. It is a least a thought that the owlet frogmouths
occupy a position in the Papuan-Australian region comparable to
that held by the smaller and chiefly insectivorous owls found
elsewhere. It may also be no accident that there are five species of
owlet frogmouths, or owlet nightjars, in Australasia. These are
diminutive, rather dumpy birds belonging to the Caprimulgiformes,
and superficially appear very similar to owls because of their upright
posture. Their habit of hawking for insects has led to them being
popularly named 'moth owls', and indeed they do resemble pigmy
owls, as well as taking most of their food on the ground, as do owls.
It may be recalled that the scops and pigmy owls are notably absent
from Australia, and the smallest *Ninox* species of that continent are
the barking and spotted hawk owls, which reach about 12in (35cm)
in length. It is at least a thought that the owlet frogmouths occupy
a position in the Papuan-Australian region comparable with that held
by smaller, chiefly insectivorous, owls found elsewhere.

Apart from the bats and other night birds, owls have to share
their world with many kinds of small terrestrial killers, all seeking
the same kind of food. As both owls and mammals take most of
their food on the ground competition is inevitable, although mammals
undoubtedly employ their keen sense of smell, as well as vision and
hearing, to root out their prey and can probably hunt in places quite
inaccessible to avian predators. In the northern fjells and tundras,
lemmings are sought by snowy owl and Arctic fox alike. Elsewhere

a host of beady-eyed carnivores like weasels, stoats and martens cover the ground beneath the staring, silent owls. Even shrews may take worms and beetles in places likely to be hunted by owls.

Perhaps the most interesting opportunity the owls have seized in the course of their sixty-million-year history has been to turn to fish as a main source of sustenance. Tawny owls will snatch fish occasionally from streams, ponds, and even back-garden goldfish tanks, but there are seven species in particular which are specially well equipped to hunt these slippery customers more efficiently than other owls. The fishing owls are chiefly, if not exclusively, nocturnal in their habits. Hearing is probably less useful than sight in catching fish lying just below the surface of the water, and none of these owls has extensive facial discs. Like the ospreys, fishing and sea eagles, the fishing owls stoop for their prey, scooping it from under the surface with their talons. These are exceedingly sharp and well developed, and the under surfaces of their feet are covered with rough and sharp spicules to help the owls secure a grip on the fish through the slime and loose scales, all features similar to those of their hawk counterparts. In the fish-hunting species, the tarsi and toes are lacking feathers, which would tend to become fouled with slime and fish scales.

Fishing owls are found in both Africa and Asia. Four Asian species (Malay, Blakistons, the brown and the tawny) all belong to the genus *Ketupa*, an array of powerful and impressive owls that may grow up to a height of 22in (55cm). All are eared, with short blunt wings nicely adapted for weaving among the trees. In fact, they have an overall appearance of 'eagle' owls but with harder plumage and relatively exposed strong bills. The three African species of *Scotopelia* are quite different, although no less distinctive than the *Ketupa* owls in appearance. None of them has ear-tufts, although they do have large round heads. Pel's is the most widespread in Africa, and lives not only in tropical rain forest, but also in most of the wooded areas of tropical Africa. The vermiculated and rufus fishing owls are restricted to equatorial Africa. As owls go, the African fishing owls are brightly coloured. Pel's is an overall orange-brown and sienna, whereas the rufus owl is really quite a bright rufus colour. The Asiatic species likewise tend towards cinnamon in parts of their ranges. Oddly enough, none of the fishing owls has evolved plumage that would make them inconspicuous against the sky to fish, whereas many plunge-diving birds have white underparts and heads, and white leading edges to their wings—as with many gulls, terns and fish-eating hawks.

In their adaptive radiation, some owls have gone back into the day to make their living, and this has enabled them to exploit sources of food, such as fish, which would probably be beyond the capability of purely nocturnal species. During the summer, all those that live in the high northern taiga and tundra areas must, of necessity, hunt by day, because either the sun never sets or else the daytime brightness is broken only by twilight periods of varying length and luminescence, depending upon the latitude. At least twelve kinds of owls may have to take to the air in full daylight because of this geographical consideration. Perhaps the snowy owl is best known as

Malay fishing owl

a diurnal species, although its neighbours, the hawk, Lapland or great gray, boreal (or Tengmalm's, as it is called in Europe), short- and long-eared owls are likewise circumpolar in their distribution and occur in high latitudes. The 6in (15cm) long pigmy, and its goliath cousin, the eagle owl of Eurasia, must also live by day and twilight in parts of their range, as does the great horned in northern Canada and Alaska.

Even species which are regarded as strictly nocturnal by most people inhabit areas which never know the dark cloak of night in summer. No species could be more nocturnal than the tawny owl, and yet these birds are found beyond latitude 60 degrees N in Norway, Finland and Sweden. Apart from the small-eyed Lapland owl, two other members of the genus *Strix* must also adapt to day or twilight conditions in the northern parts of their home ranges; the Ural owl replaces the tawny in the cold deciduous and pine forests stretching from Scandinavia to Korea. Although strictly a night flyer, this owl must be forced to hunt by day over a great swathe of countryside from Scandinavia to Siberia. In North America, barred owls may be seen on the wing during the breeding season when nests of hungry owlets demand a never-ending supply of food. Saw-whet owls, cousins of the boreal owl, are reputed to leave their roosts to hunt by day or dusk when prompted by hunger.

Apart from these species, other owls are less committed to a nocturnal way of life; the burrowing owl operates by day, and all thirteen pigmy owls of the genus *Glaucidium* are diurnal; these are like tiny hawks, speedy in flight, and will kill birds as large as themselves. Their long tails and hard-plumaged wings are not 'silenced' like those of their more nocturnal relatives.

Small perching birds are much in evidence by day, and are exploited by a number of owls. The dusky eagle owl attacks crows and has been described as a notorious egg thief, too, in the breeding season. Bird roosts are also sometimes raided by owls; they form convenient larders, and as the birds are then less alert than usual and liable to be confused in the poor light, they are easily taken. Suburban tawny owls, as mentioned in an earlier chapter, subsist to a large extent upon birds, using their wings to beat them out of the foliage, and these make up a considerable proportion (up to 21 per cent) of the food of the long-eared owls as well. In Iraq, one investigation of

this species, owls which were inhabiting date palms alongside a canal running between the Tigris and the Euphrates, revealed that birds constituted 51 per cent of the diet. Apart from house sparrows, the remains of crested larks featured in the pellets and these birds must have been killed on the ground.

The owl family's design for a diurnal falcon, or larger Accipitrine hawk, is the hawk owl. Less well equipped for hunting silently at night, this circumpolar owl has long, pointed wings and tail, and the

Young Tengmalm's owls (*Norman Olsen/Aquila Photographics*)

facial discs, so often correlated with sensitive hearing, are not so obvious. The similarity to diurnal birds of prey is heightened by the hawk owl's colour scheme, with its transverse bars on the breast and belly. It hunts in broad daylight, flying close to the ground and dropping on to small rodents, but sometimes it will survey an area hovering like a kestrel. Birds are only taken in any numbers in winter when hawk owls follow parties of willow grouse or ptarmigan.

The three little owls (*Athene*), although described as diurnal, tend to hunt most actively around dawn and dusk. In Australasia, the *Ninox* owls are both nocturnal and diurnal. The seven kinds of Afro-Asian fishing owls are also day birds. If all twenty-nine *Glaucidium* and *Ninox* owls are included, no less than fifty-three out of the 133 species now living, habitually hunt by day or by dusk over whole or parts of their home ranges; this represents two out of every five species.

Owls, then, have been singularly successful as a family in evolving more or less completely diurnal species, as well as all-purpose ones which can, if necessary, hunt both by day, in competition with hawks and falcons, and at night. In this respect owls have been more enterprising than the Falconiformes, which have clearly been unable to break the monopoly of the solely nocturnal kinds of owls and nightjars on the night scene; the bat kite is the only hawk capable of hunting after twilight and has exploited a role which no owl anywhere has yet assumed. It might be of interest here to note that the suggestion has been made that the barn owls are specialised nocturnal falcons, and not closely related to the other owls. This theory is not, however, taken too seriously in ornithological circles at present.

If further comparisons are to be drawn between the owls and the hawks, it must be conceded that the latter show a much greater range of adaptation to feeding than the former. Although the forest eagle owl of India has been observed eating the remains of goats and tigers, the owls have not produced any specialist carrion feeders like the vultures, whose relatively bare necks and faces, although macabre to our eyes, are highly functional since long feathers on the fore parts would quickly becomes matted and infested with bacteria from the messy carcases on which they feed. Presumably, nocturnal owl scavengers would have been in direct competition with mammals such as wolves, jackals, coyotes, foxes and badgers, and these could more easily locate corpses by their smell. Thus no nocturnal soaring owl would appear to be, on the basis of present-day species, a practical proposition, and soaring and carrion-feeding seem to be linked in the diurnal birds of prey. Soaring is presumably a means of extending the range of vision, but the eyes of owls are nowhere near sensitive enough at night to detect prey at long range, and the thermal activity required for effortless climbing and gliding is much less at night than in the daytime. Which explains why owls are either sitters, watching a small area of ground at close range, or flying scanners, quartering the ground at a low height.

Apart from the vultures and condors, there are hawks which have become specialist feeders on snails and snakes, raiders of nests of bees and wasps, bone droppers, interceptors, and hawkers of insects; there is even one species, the vulturine fishing eagle, which spends much of its time gorging on the seeds of the oil palm. All of these specialisations are reflected in structural modifications which have no counterpart in owls. Admittedly, the majority of the hawks, like the owls, are fairly opportunist and will take the full range of prey within their capacity to catch; but within the Falconiformes the extremes of form and function are greater than in owls. Besides which, practically all owls, even the fish-catching species, look unmistakably like owls, with the possible exception of the hawk owl which, through convergent evolution, has come to resemble a falcon and, with less conservative tastes than the specialist bird-eating peregrines, even to behave like one. Among the diurnal birds of prey, however, the long, stilt-legged secretary birds, stalking snakes beneath the soaring vultures of the African savannah, differ more from each other than any of the owls differ among themselves, and yet both of the former are classified as members of the Falconiformes.

Owls have achieved what few others have managed. They have evolved a prey-detection mechanism involving the interplay of two sensory systems, and this has made available a whole range of ground-living prey animals for the taking, animals which had become nocturnal to escape the daytime predators. Some owls, of course, depend less on hearing than others, but nevertheless the success of these birds was assured. There is no part of the land, other than Antarctica, which is not covered by the tuned ears and piercing eyes of some owl, and when the cloak of night sweeps over the earth it is the signal for countless millions of small animals to tread softly and to beware of the shadow that drops like a stone and can throttle life in an instant. The fact that millions of owls meet each dawn with their bellies full and their hunger satisfied, eloquently testifies to the effectiveness of their design for the darkness, a design which has some sixty million generations of testing, adaptation and modification behind it.

6 Owls–the Unnatural History

In the beginning, owls were unclean. The Lord spoke to Moses and itemised those creatures which should and should not be eaten by man. Cleanly creatures were cloven-hoofed and cud-chewing, finned or scaled, with some exceptions. Generally speaking, birds were clean with the exception of the predators:

> . . . These are they which ye shall have in abomination among the fowls; they shall not be eaten, they are an abomination: the eagle, and the ossifrage, and the ospray,
> . . . And the owl, and the night hawk, and the cuckow, and the hawk after his kind.
> And the little owl, and the cormorant, and the great owl. . . .
>
> *Leviticus 11, 13–17*

In biblical terms, 'unclean' animals are those whose food consists of carrion or flesh, and which are seen around dead bodies or in desolate places. Owls, seen by the Hebrew at close range, and perhaps as birds which find derelict buildings agreeable for nesting purposes, were prime candidates for uncleanness. Because of their predilection for ruins, they also served as symbols of imminent destruction. When the prophets were predicting the overthrow of Babylon they said:

> It shall never be inhabited . . . but wild beasts of the desert shall lie there; and their houses shall be full of doleful creatures; and owls shall dwell there, and satyrs shall dance there.
>
> *Isaiah 14, 20—21*

Owls also figure prominently in biblical scenes of destruction and ruination, as for example:

> The cormorant and the bittern shall possess it; the owl also and the raven shall dwell in it: and he shall stretch out upon it the line of confusion, and the stones of emptiness. . . .
>
> And thorns shall come up in her palaces, nettles and brambles in the fortresses thereof: and it shall be an habitation of dragons, and a court for owls.
>
> The wild beasts of the desert shall also meet with the wild beasts of the island, and the satyr shall cry to his fellow; the screech owl also shall rest there, and find for herself a place of rest.
>
> There shall the great owl make her nest, and lay, and hatch, and gather under her shadow: there shall the vultures also be gathered, every one with her mate.
>
> *Isaiah 34, 11—15*

The revised standard version of the Bible introduces confusion by translating *bath yannah* as ostrich, but derelict buildings and ruins generally are hardly a likely habitat for the ostrich. Dr G.R. Driver, with David Lack, has sought to bring some order into biblical bird confusion and published a table of his interpretations in the *Palestine Exploration Quarterly* of April 1955:

Hebrew name	Authorised	Revised standard version	Dr Driver
bath yannah	owl	ostrich	eagle owl

tachmas	night hawk	night hawk	short-eared owl
shachaph	cuckoo	seagull	long-eared owl
kos	little owl	owl	tawny owl
shelak	cormorant	cormorant	fisher owl
yanshuph	great owl	ibis	screech owl
tishemeth	swan	water hen	little owl
gaath	pelican	pelican	scops owl

One of the best-known folktales about the owl is the story of the baker's daughter who was turned into an owl after eating the bread her mother had baked for Jesus. According to the Gloucestershire version, Our Saviour went into a baker's shop for something to eat. The mistress put a cake in the oven for Him, but her daughter said it was too large and reduced it by half. The dough, however, swelled to an enormous size, and the daughter crying out, 'Heugh, heugh, heugh,' was transformed into an owl.

> Well, God 'ild you? They say the owl was a baker's daughter.
> Lord, we know what we are, but know not what we may be.
> God be at your table.

Hamlet, Act IV Sc. V, 41

A Spanish legend has it that the owl was once the sweetest of singers but, having been present when Jesus died, it has ever since shunned daylight and now only repeats the words 'cruz, cruz' (cross).

Owls and the Greeks

Greek religion was decidedly more anthropomorphic than that of the Egyptians. The deities tended to take over the qualities of their chosen birds and subordinate them to their own personalities. Athene was first represented by the crow, but subsequently found the owl a choicer image. At her birth 'mightily quaked great Mount Olympus beneath the weight of the owl-eyed maiden. Deeply rumbled the earth all round, and raging rose the sea in the riot of the purple waves'. Although first known as a storm and lightning goddess, Athene soon lost these meteorological characters and became a warrior goddess of great wisdom. She is sometimes portrayed with an owl head, sometimes wearing a helmet decorated with an owl symbol.

The little owl (*Athene noctua*) is, of course, named after Athene and, because of its abundance around that city, there evolved the proverb 'to take owls to Athens', similar to our 'taking coals to Newcastle'. Athenian coins bore the head of the goddess on one side and the owl on the other, and these coins were known as 'owls'.

Owls and the Romans

The Romans borrowed the owl from the Greeks and the goddess Athene became Minerva. And, sadly, the owl image altered. Pliny says:

> The scritch-owle betokeneth always some heavy news, and is most execrable and accursed in the presaging of public affairs. He keepeth ever in the deserts and loveth not only such unpeopled places, but also that are horribly hard of access. In sum, he is the very monster of the night, neither crying nor singing out clear, but uttering a certain groan of doleful moaning. And, therefore, if he be seen either within cities or otherwise abroad in any place, it is not for good, but prognosticates some fearful misfortune.

The screech owl, *Striges*, was the Roman name for a witch. In *De Proprietatibus Rerum*, by Berthelet, there is another reference to the ill omen of owls seen inside the city limits.

> Of the Owl. Diviners tell that they betoken evil; for if the owl be seen in a city, it signifieth destruction and waste. The crying of the owl by night tokeneth death.

And when an owl strayed by chance into the Capitol, the Romans underwent a formal evil-averting lustration.

> The Roman senate, when within
> The city wall an owl was seen,
> Did cause their clergy, with lustrations,
> The round-faced prodigy t'avert
> From doing town or country hurt.
>
> > *Hudibras* p ii, canto iii, Butler

Owls were bad news. To hear the hoot of an owl was to know of an imminent death. Augustus's death was thus predicted; and

Young little owls awaiting food from parents (*Joe B. Blossom*)

before the Emperor Commodus Aurelius died, an owl came and sat in his room. The murder of Caesar was also preceded by the scritching of owls.

When Agrippa, who had fallen into disfavour with Tiberius, was arrested at Capreae, an eagle owl was sitting on the branches of the tree to which he was tied. A German augur, who was present, prophesied that he would be released and would become King of the Jews—adding, however, that when he saw that owl again his death would be near. And so it came to pass; for, when sitting on his throne in state at Caesarea, he cast his eyes upwards and saw an owl perched on one of the cords which ran across the theatre. Recognising the portent of ill, he fell back smitten with disease, and in five days was dead.

Yet owls could bring a breath of hope in the form of eternal life, and in some parts of the world it was believed that the soul became united with an owl after death. In Southern Australia, tribal life was much bound up with animals, but especially were men represented by bats and women by owls. Since no one knew exactly which owl guarded a particular soul, all owls were effectively protected . . . 'if my sister Mary's life is an owl, then the owl's my sister and Mary is an owl.'

An owl preserved the life of Genghis Khan, in a manner strongly reminiscent of Robert Bruce and the spider. Pennant says:

> The Tartars and natives almost pay the owl divine honours, because they attribute to this species the preservation of the founder of their empire, Genghis Khan. That prince, with his small army, happened to be surprised and put to flight by his enemies, and forced to conceal himself in a little coppice: an owl settled on the bush under which he was hid and induced his pursuers not to search there, as they thought it impossible that any man could be concealed in a place where that bird would perch. From thenceforth they held it to be sacred, and everyone wore a plume of the feathers of this species on his head. To this day the Kalmucs continue the custom on all great festivals; and some tribes have an idol in the form of an owl, . to which they fasten the real legs of one.

The ancient Arabs believed that owls represented the souls of people who had died unavenged. Also that blood must be expiated by blood. One who had been murdered would thus crave the blood of his murderer, and in owl form he would cry out continually 'Give me to drink', until vengeance had been done. The dead were referred to as *Hàma* (skull) and the voice of the departed as *Sadã* (echo). Skull and Echo came to be names for the ghostly bird, the owl, that cries for vengeance.

When Ethiopians wished to pronounce sentence of death they carried the condemned person to a table on which an owl was painted. When the guilty man saw this he was expected to destroy himself with his own hand.

The funeral bird, monster of the night

Almost without exception, the poets have found our poor owl a dismal creature. 'Birds of omen, dark and foul, night-crow, raven, bat and owl' (Scott). They invariably use words like grave, solemn, sad, sobbing, wailing, moping, dull, moody, sullen, dismal, hoarse, grim, boding, spectral, ghostly, curst. As a universally acknowledged messenger of death, the owl calls away the soul. If the cry is dull and indistinct a near neighbour will die; if clear and distinct, then a person far away.

> The jelous swan, ayenst hys deth that singeth,
> The oule eke, that of deth the bode bringeth.
>
> *Assembly of Foules*, Folio 235, Chaucer

> Sweet Suffolk owl, so trimly dight,
> With feathers like a lady bright,
> Thou singest alone, sitting by night,
>   Te whit, te whoo, te whit, to whit.
> Thy note, that forth so freely rolls,
> With shrill command the mouse controls,
> And sings a dirge for dying souls,
>   Te whit, te whoo, te whit, to whit.
>
> *Anon*

> The scritch-owl, scritching loud,
> Puts the wretch that lies in woe
> In remembrance of a shroud.
>
> *Shakespeare*

It was the owl that shrieked, the fatal bellman
Which gives the stern'st goodnight.

Macbeth

The owl shrieked at thy birth, an evil sign.

Henry VI, Part 3

In Sicily, the 'horned' owl is especially feared. It sings near the house of a sick man three days before his death; if there are no sick people in the house, it announces to at least one of its inhabitants that he or she will be struck with squinancy of the tonsil. And in Shetland the old women say that a cow will give bloody milk if frightened by an owl, and will fall sick and die if touched by it.

While the owl clearly presides at our departing, it is also involved in our arriving. Hooting nearby could mean loss of virginity to a Welsh girl, and during her pregnancy the same sound foretells the birth of a girl. This belief is also held in the South of France, where a girl-child is foretold by the shrieking of a barn owl perched on the chimney (but a pinch of salt thrown into the fire when the owl cries will counteract any evil effects). Since the majority of births and deaths take place during the hours of darkness, it is easy enough to understand how the owl has becomes involved with these events. But why is the owl a night-bird, anyway?

One possible explanation comes from Brittany:

Once upon a time all the birds each gave one of their feathers to the wren, who had lost his own; the owl alone refused to take part in this act of charity. 'I', he said, 'will never give up a single feather, the winter is coming on and I fear the cold. 'Very well,' replied the King. 'You, Owl, from this day forward shall be the most wretched of birds. You shall always be shivering with cold, you shall never leave your abode but by night, and if you are daring enough to show yourself in the daytime the other birds shall pursue and persecute thee unsparingly.' And from that time the owl has never ceased to cry 'Hou! hou! hou!' as if he were nearly dead with cold.

A central European version goes:

The birds, wishing to procure for themselves a king, determined that whichever of them could fly the highest should be selected. The eagle had succeeded in the task, but when he was tired, the wren, who had perched on his tail, rose up and flew yet higher. For this deceit he was confined in a mousehole, and the owl appointed to guard the entrance. But whilst the other birds were taking counsel as to the punishment to be inflicted, the owl went to sleep and the prisoner escaped. Never since has the owl dared to appear in the daytime.

She is a bird indeed; but being conscious of her crime she avoids the human gaze and the light, and conceals her shame in the darkness; and by all the birds she is expelled entirely from the sky.

Ovid

Certainly, when the nocturnal owl is discovered by day by other birds, he suffers the indignity of being mobbed. So he spends the day sequestered in some quiet place, very often in an ivy bush.

And, like an owle, by night to go abroad,
Roosted all day within an ivy tod.

Dayton

Twilight, or dimpsey as Westcountrymen like to say, is the proper time for owls to be seen abroad. The seaman-poet Taylor says:

When straight we all leap overboard in haste,
Some to the knees, and some up to the waist,
Where suddenly, 'twixt owl light and the dark,
We plucked the boat beyond high-water mark.

And here is an account, taken from the *Transactions* of the Norfolk and Norwich Naturalists' Society in 1907, which shows that owls may manufacture their own light if necessary.

There are two birds, almost certainly owls, in this district (North Norfolk) which exhibit a hitherto unrecorded phenomenon. I am inclined to believe that most of the tales respecting 'will-of-the-wisps', 'corpse-candles', and 'lantern-men' are the result of occasional luminosity assumed by birds of nocturnal habits that frequently fly over marshy ground in search of prey. For instance on February 3, 1907, on reaching the top of Twyford Hill, we noticed a light apparently moving in the direction of Wood Norton, and about a quarter of a mile to the north of us. After moving horizontally backwards and forwards several hundred yards, it rose in the air to the height of forty feet or more; it then descended and again went through the same evolutions many times. The light was slightly reddish in the centre, and resembled a carriage lamp for which we at first mistook it. We watched it for twenty minutes and were quite at a loss to ascertain its cause. The light emerged from a covert about two hundred yards distant, flying backwards and forwards across the field, at times approaching within fifty yards of where I was standing. It then alighted on the ground for a few seconds. A slight mist hung over the ground. On another occasion, the evening being dark, the bird issued from a covert. Its luminosity seemed to have increased, and it literally lighted up the branches of the trees as it flew past them, occasionally mounting over their tops. After watching it for about half an hour, it was joined by a companion bird hardly so bright. This kept about one hundred yards behind it, but not constantly.

I have recorded these observations merely in the hope that some naturalist may be found whose scientific attainments will enable him to elucidate the cause of a highly interesting natural phenomenon, and thereby refute the contemptible assertions of those who pour ridicule on everything they have not seen themselves, to the great detriment of scientific research.

The owl is a magical bird and has its human observers well and truly bewitched; it is a bird of witchcraft, death and doom.

Lizard's leg, and howlet's wing,
For a charm of powerful trouble,
Like a hell-broth boil and bubble.

Macbeth

Shakespeare's witches were careful to introduce an owlet's wing into their bubbling cauldron, because no witch's charm could be really efficacious without it. Horace's witch, Canidia, used owl plumage in her incantation:

Et uncta turpis ova ranae sanguine,
Plumamque nocturnae strigis.

Ovid, too, mentions it in referring to the potion brewed by Medea. And Ben Jonson, in his 'Masque of Queenes', sings how:

The screech owl's eggs and the feathers black,
The blood of the frog and the bone in his back,
I have been getting, and made of his skin
A purset, to keep Sir Cranion in.

If the heart and right foot of an owl are laid on a sleeping person, then he will confess all. If an owl's liver is hung on a tree, all the birds collect under it. Yet in spite of its character as a bird of ill omen, there are occasions when the owl may be regarded as bringing good fortune. If it flies into a dovecot it brings luck. Its cry may free a sufferer from fever, and its feathers bring peaceful slumber. Its appearance near the house of a pregnant woman forecasts an easy delivery, or the birth of a boy, or other good fortune. And if you detect an element of 'double-think' in all this, then be quiet about it and keep your own counsel. Think of all the useful things owls will do for you. In India, owl's flesh is an aphrodisiac, although at the same time it may cause you to become a fool and lose your memory. On the other hand, eating the eyeballs of an owl gives the power of seeing in the dark. The English version of this requires you to eat owls' eggs, charred and powdered.

In Yorkshire, it was believed that owl broth was a cure for whooping-cough. Cyranides declared that soup made from owls' eggs, while the moon was waning, would cure epilepsy. In many parts of Europe an owl's egg was said to be a sure cure for drunkenness, or, prevention being better than a cure, to give an owl's egg to a child was to ensure that he would never become a drunkard. A prescription of ancient medicine was that the eggs of an owl, if drunk for three days in wine, made drunkards abstemious, while Philostratos, in the 'Life of Apollonius', says that by eating an owl's egg one acquires a dislike for wine before having tasted it. Pliny, of course, knew all the owl's properties but he brought his cold scientific eye to bear on them.

The feet of a scritch owl burnt together with the herb Plumbago, is very good against serpents. But before I write further of this bird, I cannot pass over the vanity of Magicians which herein appeareth most evidently; for over and besides many other monstrous lies which they have devised, they give it out that if one do lay the heart of a scritch-owl on the left pap of a woman as she lies asleep, she will disclose and utter all the secrets of her heart; also, whosoever carry about them the same heart when they go to fight, shall be more hardy, and perform their devoir the better against their enemies.

Owls' eggs were also reputed to cure all defects and accidents to the hair, but Pliny says:

I would fain know what man ever found a scritch-owl's nest and met with any of their eggs, considering that it is held for an uncouth and strange prodigy to have seen the bird itself. And what might be he that tried such conclusions and experiments, especially in the hair of his head.

Natural History

Owls in the New World

Among the American Indians, the owl was believed to lament the golden age when men and animals lived in perfect unity. When it came to pass that they quarrelled, the Great Spirit sailed in disgust across the seas, to return only when they had made up their differences. So every night in the great pine forests the snowy owl repeats his 'Koo, koo, koos'—'Oh, I am sorry, Oh, I am sorry'.

Many American tribes associate the owl with the dead; the bridge over which the dead had to pass in the Ojibwa belief was known as the owl-bridge. Kwakiute Indians believe that the owl represents both the dead person and the free soul. The owl with which the ego is united after death exists already in this life as a closely related being worthy of respect. If the owl is killed, so also is the person. So we have the concept of spiritual repetition, of a soul-bearer paving the way for further development. As a guardian spirit, the owl must be properly addressed: 'Welcome, Supernatural One, thank you for coming, trying to come to me that I may see you, long-

life-maker. Please, do not leave me and pray take good care of me
that nothing evil may befall me, long-life-maker.'

There is an American Indian version of the creation of owls:

> The husband of a young girl bought a small hut for her
> mother beside his hunting lodge. He killed many beaver, and
> while he and his wife cooked and ate the intestines, her mother
> cooked and ate the meat. The old woman, however, craved the
> intestines, because they had a lot of fat. One day she said to her
> daughter, 'Come with me and gather birch-bark for baskets.'
> They found a large birch-tree, and the mother stayed on the
> ground while the girl climbed to remove the bark. Then the
> old woman said to her, 'My daughter, say *hu hu* and fly away'.
> The girl refused, but at her mother's urging she at last said *hu
> hu* and fluttered her hands. Immediately she changed to an owl
> and flew away, only her skin remaining in the birch tree. Her
> mother then climbed the tree, put on her daughter's skin and
> returned to the camp.
>
> When the young man came back from his hunting, he
> mistook the old woman for his wife and gave her the intestine
> of a beaver to cook. When it was cooked he ate one end of it
> while she ate the other, but being toothless, her chewing made
> no noise. He said to her, 'I do not hear you eating.' And she
> answered, 'Today I was chewing birch-bark and my teeth are
> no good.' When they had finished their meal, he gave her some
> meat and told her to give it to her mother, but the old woman
> secretly threw it into the woods.
>
> After they had gone to bed, his wife flew on top of the
> house and called, '*Hu, hu*. You are sleeping with your mother-
> in-law.' The youth, who was already suspicous, realised at once
> what had happened and tried to capture his wife, calling, 'I
> love you. Come back and be my wife again.' But she answered,
> 'I cannot return, for I have already changed to an owl.' And
> she flew away among the trees. He went back and killed his
> mother-in-law, then followed after his wife entreating her to
> return to him. She said to him, 'I cannot return, my husband.
> But you too say *hu hu* and fly.' As he repeated the words and

fluttered his hands, his skin also dropped from him and the two owls flew away together. Thus owls originated in the world.

Journal of American Folklore

As in Europe, the New World owl is believed to be a harbinger of death and doom. When the owl-call is heard in the woods the passer-by must challenge it to reply by repeating the note. The bird's refusal is accepted as an augury of death. But in Alabama, the correct response to the dreaded call was to take off a shoe and turn it over, when the owl would desist. Or, on hearing the owl or other bird of ill omen, the person concerned must pull off some article of clothing and put it on again wrong side out, when the bird will leave and no harm will befall. Again, if your hear an owl at night, take a broom and lay it across the door, and he will stop immediately. But, to prevent him from hooting, heat the poker red hot, as this will burn his toes and he will quit hooting to seek running water in which to cool the burn.

Owls are connected with the weather, too. Bad weather is foretold by the hooting of a horned owl. The owl was one of the names of Mictlantecutli, the Mexican Pluto whose realm of the dead was supposedly situated in the cold and dreary north. The wind from that quarter was imagined by the Chippewas to be made by the owl—and the south wind by the butterfly.

Among the Creek Indians the junior priests, or students, wear a white mantle with a great horned owl skin ingeniously stuffed to appear like the living bird. The dress has large, sparkling, glass beads fixed into the head for eyes and this insignia of divine wisdom is sometimes worn as a crest on top of the head, and at other times the image sits on the arm or is held in the hand. These bachelors are also distinguished from other people by their taciturnity, grave and solemn countenances, and dignified step. They sing songs or hymns to themselves in a low sweet voice as they stroll about the town.

The Kiowa Indians believe that a medicine man becomes an owl after death, and that the owl after death becomes a cricket.

Owls could also be the hunter's friend, and during 'possum hunting, the tawny could be relied on to give useful information. Three hoots from the left-hand side was sure warning that there'd be no 'possums, hooting from the right was the green light. And there is the tale of the starving hunter:

> Once there was a great hunter who suddenly was unable to kill anything. Moose fled from him. He used up all his dried store meat and provisions and he suffered more than his family, for he had to walk. 'I'll go off', he said to his wife, 'and die all by myself.' He could not go far since he had little tobacco. 'I wish there was someone here to smoke with me,' he said. Instantly he heard someone coming, and a fine large man with a big nose came. 'I've heard you,' he said. 'Yes, true, here's my pipe filled, I'd like to smoke with you.' They smoked. The stranger said, 'You look as though you were starved.' 'I am.' 'Never fear, follow my tracks. In the morning you will be saved.' The stranger started off. 'Now look at me,' he said, and the man did. It was an Owl. In the morning, the starving hunter quickly killed two bears and after that had abundance.

Owl proverbs

A wise old owl sat in an oak,
the more he saw the less he spoke,
the less he spoke the more he heard,
why can't we all be like that wise old bird.

Anon

The gravest fish is an oyster,
the gravest bird is an owl,
the gravest beast's an ass,
An' the gravest man is a fule.

Scottish Proverbs, John Ray, 1670

He's in great want of a bird that will give a groat for an owl.
Compleat Collection of English Proverbs, John Ray, 1670

The owl thinks all her young ones beauties.

The owl is not accounted wiser for living retiredly.
Gnomologia, Thos Fuller, 1732

It is unlucky to shoot an owl.
The Evil Eye, F.T. Elworthy, 1895

Like an owl in an ivy-bush.

> (Ivy was the favourite plant of Bacchus,
> and supposedly the favourite haunt of owls.)

I wasn't born in a wood to be scared by an owl.

Belle's Strategem, 1780

Owl slang

Owl—a harlot (obsolete 19th century).

To owl—to smuggle (c 1735-1820, an owler was a person or vessel engaged in smuggling sheep or wool from England to France).

To walk by owl-light—to fear arrest (c 1650-1700).

To owl—to sit up at night (1890s onwards, now obsolete).

Take the owl—to become angry (18th, mid-19th century).

Appendix 1

Owl Eyesight and Hearing

To understand why owls are able to see at light levels far below those required by human beings it is first necessary to consider how eyes work and what, on the whole, they are able to do. Eyes are light receptors of a very sophisticated kind concerned with producing and analysing pictures of the environment. Each eye collects light through a window, the *cornea*, and with the help of this and a dense, transparent *lens*, focuses an inverted image on to a sensitive *retina*, which then transmutes the light energy into nervous impulses. These then travel up the *optic nerve* to the analysing areas of the *visual cortex*—a part of the brain. A muscular *iris* acts like an adjustable curtain, controlling the amount of light that passes through the lens, in much the same way as the diaphragm operates in a camera. The curvature of the lens (and cornea of birds), and with it the power of the lens, can also be increased at will by the muscles of the *ciliary body*, thus bringing near objects into sharp focus; this process is called *accommodation*. The iris may also help in this business of accommodation because, when it is fully expanded and shut down (ie, when the central *pupil* is small), the eye resembles a pin-hole camera and objects both near and far are rendered in sharp detail on the retina.

Unlike the eyes of mammals, those of birds are reinforced by a ring of bony plates called *scleral ossicles*, which girdle the cornea in the tough outer layer of the eyeball. These are fused to the skull accounting for the fact that owls cannot move their eyes inside their orbits. Also projecting into the posterior chamber of the eye from the point where the optic nerve passes through the retina, is a pleated vascular structure, the *pecten*. Although smallest in nocturnal species, it may be concerned both with making the eye more sensitive to movements and with supplying oxygen and nutrients to the retina, which, in birds, is devoid of blood vessels.

The secret of the owl's good eyesight in the dark lies in the size and construction of its eyes, and these are not simply giant versions of those of its day-living cousins. Vision is concerned with two quite separate capabilities: the ability to discriminate fine details of the objects within the visual field (*visual acuity*), and the ability to perceive small quantities of light (*sensitivity*). During the daytime, there is plenty of light and so eyes possessed by diurnal animals like squirrels, marmots, ungulates and most birds, have relatively small 'windows'. Nevertheless, the amount of detail capable of resolution by the eye will obviously increase with the size of the image. In diurnal species, then, the lens tends to be flat with a long focal length, which means that a comparatively large image is brought to a focus on the retina way back from the lens. Because of the high intensity light that enters through the pupil, the consequent loss of brightness of the large image does not matter; it will still be bright enough to register on the retina. The posterior chambers of these eyes are accordingly relatively large, as anyone who has dissected the eye of a starling or swallow will have discovered.

· ·However, *visual acuity* depends not only upon the quality of the optical system and the size and sharpness of the image, but also upon the types of light-sensitive cells making up the retina, how closely they are packed together, and the way in which they are connected to the optic nerve. This is not the place to examine the structure and physiology of eyes in any detail, but suffice it to say that, in vertebrates, two types of photo-receptors can be found in retinas.

Cones are cylindrical cells which may be tapered towards their outer tips and these are relatively insensitive to light (ie, they need a high level of illumination to stimulate them) and tend to predominate in the retinas of diurnal species. Day (or *photopic*) and colour vision are mediated through the cones.

By far the most sensitive cells within the receptor layer of the retina are the *rods*. These continue to function when the level of light falling on the retina is too low to stimulate the cones, and night vision (or *scotopic* vision) is carried out through the operation of the rods. In the human eye, an all-purpose structure, the distribution of these two types of cells differs. The peripheral regions of the retina are rich in rods, whereas towards the centre, immediately behind the lens and on its optical axis, the retina is almost completely composed of cones. Consequently, at night, when the light is very poor, the retina is unable to resolve much from the central areas of the retinal image, whereas the best sensitivity is retained on the edges of the field of vision, corresponding to the parts of the image projected on to the rod-rich regions.

The ability to distinguish fine detail, or the resolving power of the retina, also depends upon how many visual cells are connected up to each optic-nerve fibre. Rods and cones carry pigments which break down when illuminated, and this photochemical process ultimately causes electrical changes in neighbouring *bipolar* cells; these are nerve cells which, in turn, stimulate *ganglion* cells, whose long axon or conducting fibres transmit electrical impulses to the brain. Ideally, each rod and cone should connect with one ganglion cell, so that each visual cell has its own private line to the brain. If, in the interests of sensitivity, more than one rod or cone were connected to a single bipolar cell, or similarly, if a number of bipolar cells were to converge on to a single ganglion cell, then visual acuity would necessarily suffer. One-to-one representation would produce for the brain a detailed picture rather like a fine-grained, good-quality photograph, whereas massive convergence, or summation, of receptor and bipolar cells would produce a vague, grainy representation of the image, similar to a highly magnified photograph produced on coarse-screened newsprint.

Cones, which are characteristic of chiefly diurnal birds' eyes, usually have their own bipolar and ganglion cells, and this explains

Little owls typically perch on posts, telegraph poles or old trees (*M. C. Wilkes/Aquila Photographics*)

why they tend also to be associated with the ability to resolve minute detail; rods tend to join forces and so animals with predominantly rod retinas tend to be highly sensitive to light at the expense of detail. Sensitivity and visual acuity, for this reason, tend to be mutually exclusive. Either an animal can read newsprint at a distance of 10ft (3m), or else it has a very useful degree of night vision with reduced amount of detail. Owls, predictably, have predominantly rod retinas, and yet, curiously enough, this seems to have been achieved at no expense to their ability to discern detail. Unlike nocturnal mammals, these birds can probably resolve as much from the night scene as we could by day; indeed, there is even evidence that owls can see better by night than we can by the light of the sun.

One of the first essentials for an eye which has to operate by night is that it must be able to collect and concentrate as much light as possible. The eyes of owls are large indeed—that of a snowy owl weighs as much as a man's eye—but size alone is not enough. The design must differ from those of diurnal species. One of the most striking features of an owl's eye is the relative size of the 'window'— the cornea and lens system; in photographers' jargon nocturnal eyes are 'fast', that is to say, size for size, they are capable of letting in far more light than diurnal ones. In practical terms, a 'fast' lens is *wider* than a slow one (eg, compare the size of the lens of a camera fitted with an f 1.9 as opposed to an f 2.8 lens), and when there is not enough light for the latter to operate, the former can still collect enough to throw a bright image on to the film. The same analogy can be drawn between the eyes of owls and day birds.

Since an owl's eye has a large, fast cornea and lens, the system would tend to throw a large image a long way back, with consequent loss of brightness, were it not that rounder and more powerful lenses have been evolved to bring the image back closer to the lens, and the resultant retention of brightness is just what nocturnal birds require. Thus, when man and owl survey the same night scene, the difference between the brightness of the images on their respective retinas goes a long way to explain why one can only stumble and

The great gray is the largest North American owl (*Wayne Lankinen/Aquila Photographics*)

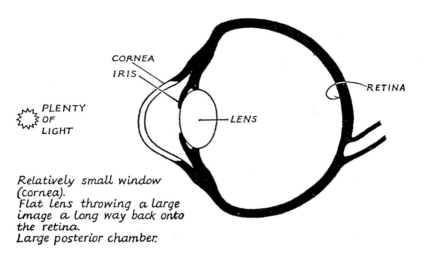

PLENTY
OF
LIGHT

CORNEA

IRIS

LENS

RETINA

Relatively small window
(cornea).
Flat lens throwing a large
image a long way back onto
the retina.
Large posterior chamber.

EYE FOR THE NIGHT-TIME HUNTER

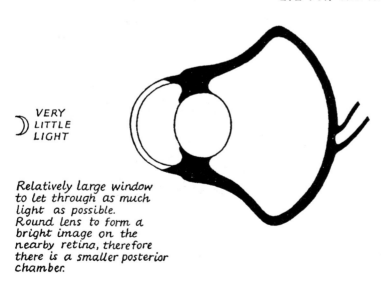

VERY
LITTLE
LIGHT

Relatively large window
to let through as much
light as possible.
Round lens to form a
bright image on the
nearby retina, therefore
there is a smaller posterior
chamber.

SECTIONS THROUGH TWO TYPES OF AVIAN EYE

grope, while the other can weave in and out of the trees with no trouble at all. The optics of their system, together with the fact that they have highly sensitive rod-rich retinas, means that, without any further sophistications, owls are well equipped to probe the darkest nooks by night.

There is, however, yet another way of making better use of the amount of light that enters the eye. In diurnal birds and mammals, the back of the eye is heavily pigmented to prevent reflections that would blur the image thrown on to the retina. In nocturnal mammals and probably owls, there is a reflecting structure called the *tapetum*, which ensures that any light unabsorbed by the receptor cells has a second change of stimulating the rods as it is reflected back through the eye; this accounts for the eye-shine of cats, bush babies, ungulates and even whales. Furthermore, in eyes made to function well at night, there may be several layers of receptor cells to increase the chances of catching every available beam of light.

A popular misconception is that owls are blind by daylight. This is patently untrue; after all, some species hunt by day, and eagle owls have been found to possess vision more acute than we have by day. Nevertheless, the relatively enormous tubular eyes of these birds,

In bright light the pale yellow iris of the little owl contracts, allowing little light through the pupil onto the sensitive retina. At night it opens to allow in as much light as possible.

tuned for night life, are highly sensitive pieces of equipment, and must be protected against the glare of daylight. It is the function of the muscular iris to keep the amount of light passing through the lens to an optimum; should too much shine through on to the back of the eye, the retina could be damaged with consequent blindness. As the eyes of owls have to operate both by day and night, the range of adjustment called for by the iris must be correspondingly enormous. When dark-adapted, this light shield is drawn right back, and in species which have yellow or orange irises, these are reduced to thin, narrow rings surrounding the shiny black pupils, a position in which the lens is exposed to catch every possible ray of light. By day, the iris muscles constrict to shut down the exposure of the sensitive retina.

Owls have spherical pupils, and in this respect their eyes are designed for twenty-four-hours vision, whereas many nocturnal animals whose eyes are probably more sensitive (if not as discerning of detail) than those of owls, have vertical slits which, unlike circular irises, can be all but shut by day. By day, the cat, for example, may have pupils reduced to two tiny pin-points, and some geckos peep at the sun-lit world through three minute apertures in each eye. In owls, the opaque nictitating membrane (a kind of in-built sunglasses!) also helps to shield their eyes, and it is possible that a migration of light-absorbing black pigment into the receptors of the retina may help to cut down the amount of light reaching the rods, thus preventing damage.

Even so, the rods and cones themselves can become more or less sensitive over a short period of time, a process known as adaptation. Cones, however, are far less adaptable than rods, and a predominantly rod retina, such as is possessed by owls, is a thousand times more sensitive to light when fully adapted than a pure cone one. It is not, therefore, true that diurnal birds are blind at night; their sight is as good as ours, but it might take them perhaps an hour to get used to the darkness and have useful sight, whereas it takes us, with our round-the-clock visual apparatus, ten minutes or so. Owls presumably develop maximum sensitivity even more quickly.

It is always difficult to prove whether an animal can perceive colour. As owls have some cones in their retina, it seems likely that they can do so when the light is good—like diurnal birds whose colour vision is second to none in the animal kingdom. However, experiments on a crepuscular little owl, which was taught to distinguish colours against a series of greys matched for their luminance, showed beyond reasonable doubt that it could perceive yellow, green and blue; red and the darkest grey were confused.

The tubular form of owls' eyes has been evolved presumably to save space inside the skull, but the effects of their curious shape is not without interest. Most birds have a small but limited eye movement within their sockets but owls' eyes, because of their tubular construction, are not capable of rotary movements. Owls, however, make up for their fixed eyes by having exceptionally mobile necks; the head can rotate through at least 270 degrees— which accounts for the story that, by walking round a nesting owl, you can get it to twist its head off!

Turning now to the owl's other great asset in finding its prey— its exceptionally keen hearing ability—we know that information about sounds is coded into nervous impulses by the inner ear, and that these are transmitted by the auditory nerve to that part of the brain called the *medulla*. The number of nerve cells, or *neurons*, that receive the auditory information in the medulla is a good indication as to how important ears are for each species as windows on the world. As the brain is in many ways like a processing computer, the larger the part dealing with the ear the more sophisticated is the type of analysis performed on the coded nerve impulses. Big birds, however, have bigger brains with more cells in them, so the comparison must be made with care. Nevertheless, a barn owl weighing 10½oz (300g) has no less than 95,000 neurons, whereas a carrion crow weighing *double* had only in the region of 27,000.

Thus, relatively speaking, the barn owl is far ahead of the crow in its complement of auditory analysing cells. So, too, for their size, are long-eared and tawny owls, though both the eagle and little owls, with less complicated ear structures, have the normal complements of medulla auditory neurons for birds of their size. It is at least a thought that large owls like the eagle and other big *Bubos* may hunt more by vision, because their eyes are so much larger than those of many other smaller species, and that acute hearing may, therefore, be less necessary to them. However, the Lapland or great gray owl, another large species, has relatively small eyes but enormous facial discs, possibly indicating as advanced a sense of hearing as the other *Strix* owls.

Before turning to laboratory experiments which have shown just how highly refined is the barn owl's sense of hearing, it is first necessary to consider the nature of 'sound'. Any disturbance of the air, as by the movement of vocal chords or the falling of a leaf, will set up vibrations, and waves will radiate outwards from the source of the disturbance at the rate of about 1,130ft (343m) per second, dependent upon the prevailing barometric pressure and temperature. These vibrations may be likened to ripples radiating from where a stone has been cast into a pond, and when these waves of rarefaction and compression reach the ear-drum they set it into motion, causing it to vibrate. The movements are then transmitted to the inner ear, where they are analysed and perceived as sounds. The rate of vibration, as measured by the numbers of 'waves' that hit the ear-drum each second (cycles/second or frequency), determines the pitch we hear, so that the higher the frequency the higher the pitch that is perceived. Middle C on a piano keyboard is equivalent to 262 cycles/second, and the upper limit to human hearing ranges from 15,000–20,000 cycles/second (15–20 Kh). Frequencies beyond that are referred to as *ultrasonic* (ie, beyond human hearing).

It is possible to find out in the laboratory exactly what sounds owls can hear by conditioning them to react in some way to pure sounds (ie, sounds of single frequencies). If they fail to respond when a sound is played to them, then they are presumably deaf to noises of that frequency, as we are to the ultrasonic chirps of bats. In general, it turns out that the upper limit of hearing in owls is probably similar to that of our own. Great horned owls can certainly hear well beyond 8 Kh and long-eared owls can perceive pure tones of 18 Kh; 20 Kh represents the upper limit to hearing in the barn owl. Owls may, however, be less sensitive to low frequencies than we are; 100 c.p.s. (0.1 Kh) seems to be the lower limit for the long-eared and tawny although the great horned owl hears sounds as low as 60 c.p.s. (0.06 Kh). With this sound window, they would be completely oblivious of the rich notes played on the lower octave of the piano, and instruments like the double bass or certain registers on the organ would be as meaningless to them as a dog's whistle is to us.

The range of hearing is not, however, the only measurement by which this sense of an animal may be assessed; it is also necessary to know the sensitivity of the ear mechanism to different tones and intensities. This is a measure of its tuning, and can be determined, for example, by playing a sound of known frequency, starting softly and increasing its volume until the owl responds. For some sounds, a response can be measured when the volume is so low that it remains almost imperceptible to us, whereas for others the owl may remain quite deaf to it until the volume is turned up considerably.

Experimental work carried out at the Free University of Amsterdam by Dr van Dijk has revealed that tawny and long-eared owls, both species with large external ear openings, can hear low (2 Kh) and medium (6 Kh) frequency notes about ten times better than we can; in other words, they can detect sounds of this order that are too soft for us to perceive. In this respect, owls have similar hearing to that of cats, although small cats are able to out-perform barn owls in their perception of sound above 10 Kh. For the tawny owl, the range of maximum sensitivity lies between 3 and 6 Kh, and for the long-eared owls about 6 Kh. By comparison, the great horned owl is more sensitive to lower-pitched sounds of about 1 Kh, as indeed we are ourselves.

Another feature of the owl's anatomy must also be explained; the fact that the ears and their attendant flaps are asymmetrical. Although the great gray owl has ear openings of approximately the same length, other owls can have as much as 50 per cent difference between their external ears—the right ear usually being the longest. How does this alter their perception of sounds and how does it help them to locate their food? Roger Payne investigated this problem at Cornell University by implanting microphones in the ears of barn owls and measuring the sound intensities at the sites of the ear-drums while broadcasting sounds of constant volume from various angles. From his data, it appeared that barn owls were able to hear certain sounds better in certain directions than in others. According to Dr Payne:

> At about 5 Kh, each ear has a broad region of maximum sensitivity directed forward with sensitivity falling off gradually as a sound is directed at either side of the head. As the frequency is raised, the region of maximum sensitivity becomes narrower.   .   .   .

Sounds above 5 Kh up to 15 Kh will always be *heard* loudest when they come from the direction of the line of sight; the higher the sound is pitched, the more clearly will the ears pick it up from a direction pointing almost straight ahead. So, providing a barn owl orientates its head so that it receives high-pitched sounds (ie, approaching 15 Kh) equally loudly in both ears, it should then be staring its next meal straight in the face!

There are still further refinements. The asymmetry of the ears means that the 'sound window', or the hearing on one side of the head, is the mirror image of that on the other, *except* that the right one is displaced 10–15 degrees higher than that on the left-hand side. In practice, this means that if a sound source (say, a rodent) moves away from the line of sight while the owl's head remains stationary, the reception in one ear will decrease with extreme rapidity while it will do so more slowly, or may even increase, in the other. Differences arising out of the incorrect orientation of the head are thereby amplified, and corrective realignment is made all the more easily.

Owls, of course, do not hunt entirely blind, and the ears and eyes form part of the highly sophisticated detection system that contributes in no small measure to the hunting prowess of these birds after dark. As more species are critically studied in the laboratories, it will probably be found that the extraordinary hearing of the barn owl is common to those species with well-developed facial discs and outer-ear structures.

An interesting fact about owls has come to light through the researches of Professor Karel Voous, a Dutch ornithologist. For a long time owls had been classified according to the complexity, size and degree of asymmetry in their ears and associated flaps. Eagle and scops owls, for example, have small ear openings and no marked asymmetry, and these and their kin have been termed *bubonine* owls. On the other hand, *strigine* owls are characterised by the extreme development of asymmetry and large ear openings. The division was always considered fundamental. Professor Voous challenged this assumption on the grounds that their hearing, reflected in the complexity of the ears, might be a highly variable feature within closely related sorts of owls, because, after all, the usefulness of sound in prey location might vary from place to place, or from species to species, depending upon their chief sources of food.

In support of this theory, Professor Voous took ear measurements of some wood owls (*Strix* and *Ciccaba* species), ranging from tropical ones to those that live in the northern temperate and cooler coniferous forests. He found that the size of the ears (measured as the total of the mean lengths of both left and right ears) increased from tropical to sub-Arctic habitats. The African Woodford's owl had a total ear length of less than half that of the Ural owl (23mm as opposed to 51mm). Similarly, the mean width of the ear flaps increased with latitude; tropical and sub-tropical species of *Strix* and *Ciccaba* had flaps that varied between 1 and 7mm in width (*C. nigrolineata* had no flaps at all) whereas the Ural owl's was 13mm. The more temperate tawny had ear flaps on average only 9.5mm wide. The great gray owl had ears to match its name, with a total of 54mm of ear opening (right and left) and with 15mm ear flaps. Oddly enough, the tropical and sub-tropical species tended to have a greater degree of asymmetry (with a ratio of 100:152 in the case of *Ciccaba virgata* as opposed to 100:114 in the Ural owl), possibly because in the northern owls *both* ear openings approached the maximum possible for the size of their owners' heads.

If size, then, is anything to go by, hearing is much better developed in the northern owls than in their closely related tropical cousins. Professor Voous concludes that:

> locating the high squeaks of mammalian prey in lonely and generally silent, long sub-Arctic nights by great powers of hearing helped by a movable, dermal ear flap may be as great a necessity for the life of northern strigine owls as it probably is misleading to the southern ciccabine owls in the chirping and creaking chorus of stridulent insects and peeping frogs that make the nights in many tropical areas at times ear-deafening.

Appendix 2

Owls in Boxes

Owls will use artificial nest-sites readily, and should be most welcome residents at any suitable habitat. The domestic cat has had a good run for its money, partly on account of its mouse-catching qualities. Why should we not equally encourage an owl to join us?

The first requirement is that the terrain should be suitable for the species you propose to attract: well-wooded farm, parkland or gardens for the tawny owl, or fields, open country and marsh for the barn owl. Breeding success depends to a large extent on the availability or otherwise of natural sites, such as decayed trees (tawny) or derelict buildings (barn), but if you site your nestbox cleverly you always stand a chance.

For tawny owls you must have a box of the enclosed type, 30in (76cm) inside depth, floor 8in (20cm) square, and with an 8in (20cm) diameter entrance hole near the top (see illustration). Give it a wide roof, with a good overlap, waterproofed with roofing felt. If you want to be able to look in and inspect the contents, you may need an inspection port near the bottom of the box, but a word of warning is appropriate—tawny owls are notorious for 'having a go'. The male bird, especially, is likely to attack you, so it is important to have a pane of glass inside the inspection hatch.

Fix the box fairly high up a convenient tree, giving it shelter from the noonday sun, if necessary, and avoiding the damp. The actual height at which it is fixed does not seem to be very critical.

Have a convenient perch of some kind fairly near the entrance hole. When the juvenile birds first leave the nest they will appreciate having an easy goal to aim for. At this stage their wings are surprisingly ineffective and they use their feet a good deal to get a purchase on their surroundings.

It is at this time that the juvenile birds may fall and find themselves grounded. They are good climbers and can certainly tackle a vertical tree-face. Left to themselves, they will climb to the very top of the tree every day and sit there for long periods, occasionally flexing their wings and 'playing' at flying. They are slow to fledge and this period may last several weeks.

In the wild, incidentally, tawnies do not invariably nest in tree holes. They may use second-hand crow, hawk or heron nests or squirrel dreys. Sometimes they will use barns or rocky ledges. They lay two to four white eggs in late March or early April. The incubation period is from twenty-eight to thirty days. Fledging period about four weeks. Single brood.

Barn owls require a very different kind of nest box. It should consist of an open tray 36in long, 15in wide and 12in deep (90 × 37 × 30cm). The interior should be divided into two equal areas with a partition 7 or 8in (17 or 20cm) deep (see illustration). A two-compartment apple-box should serve the purpose when you've knocked the top middle section out. The tray should be placed just inside and below a large (1 or 2ft (30/60cm) diameter) entrance hole to a suitable building, loft or recess well above the ground. The owls will nest in the section of the tray farthest from the hole. On the whole, they are disinclined to occupy sites of buildings which are already inhabited by people. Incidentally, in Germany, farmers leave

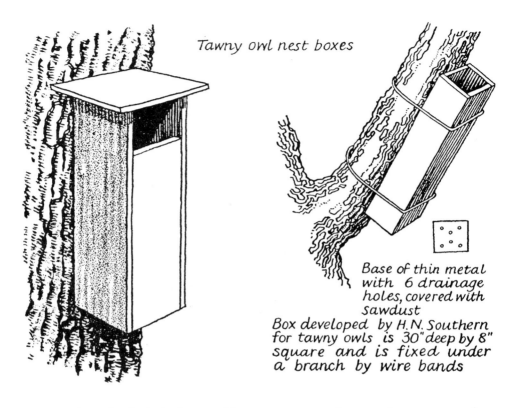

Tawny owl nest boxes

Base of thin metal
with 6 drainage
holes, covered with
sawdust
Box developed by H.N. Southern
for tawny owls is 30"deep by 8"
square and is fixed under
a branch by wire bands

a triangular hole in barn-gables to encourage barn-owls to enter and destroy mice. It is known as the *Eulenflucht.*

In the wild, barn owls look for breeding sites in the vicinity of farms, old buildings, church towers, etc. They hunt over fields, open country and marsh for small rodents and even small birds. Although semi-derelict buildings are their favourite nest sites, they will also use hollow trees and cliff crevices.

For the actual nest they use no special materials, and the four to seven white eggs are often surrounded by a pile of castings. The eggs are laid from April to July. Incubation period is thirty-two to thirty-four days; fledging about ten weeks. Unlike the tawny, barn owls often have two broods.

After the breeding season, it is as well to clean out the nest-boxes, since you'll find they are no longer lily-white and pure.

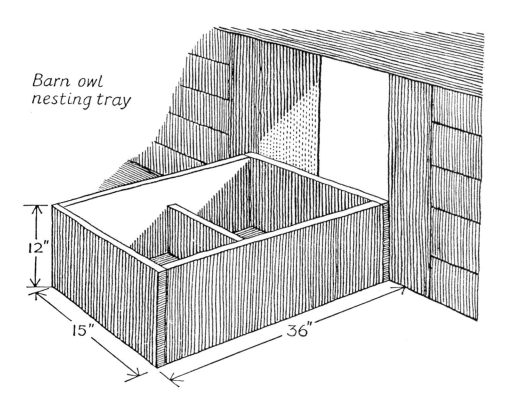

Barn owl nesting tray

12"

15"

36"

In Finland, great gray owls nest in old raptor nests and can be encouraged to nest—quite successfully—in artificially made nests.

Feeding Wild Owls

Not easy, or even necessarily desirable. It is far more important that there should be an ample supply of natural food available within the owl's hunting territory. Nevertheless, there is a certain interest in trying to persuade 'your' owl to come to the equivalent of the bird table.

The first thing is to find where the owl is roosting. Then, at a regular time every day, just before dusk, put the food on a suitable perching post fairly close. Raw meat is probably the easiest offering, but dead chicks or pigeon heads serve very well.

So far as we know, there is no trick of the trade for persuading owls to come to food. Whether or not you succeed seems to depend on luck to a large extent. It may be that the owl has to come upon the food by chance the first time.

Owls in Captivity

Owls are strictly protected and it is illegal to take them from the nest. But, of course, it often happens that an injured or lost fledgling may come your way. One of us had the unlikely-sounding experience of seeing a half-drowned juvenile barn owl fished out of a river by a fisherman who foul-hooked it with a very skilful cast. The owl survived and in due course was successfully weaned back into the wild.

A more likely course of events is that a young owl falls out of the nest-tree and is unable to climb back. When this happens your first aim should be to try to get it back to a point near the nest, when it should be able to manage without any further help. But it may be that for one reason or another you choose to take the bird home and try to hand-rear it.

Keep it in a deep box; there is no need for any kind of nest material though a small quantity of straw may make it easier for the bird to move about without slipping. The best food will be chicks (which can sometimes be obtained very easily from poultry-rearing establishments, dead-in-shell), mice, pigeon-heads, and possibly best of all, raw beef. Give voles or mice whole as soon as possible. If you feed the bird on raw beef, then it is important to vary the diet with some of the other items, because the growing owl needs roughage. The liver, heart and bones of the prey-animal are important to the owl. Although he will eat the fur of a mouse, for instance, this is not one of the important items. It is no good being squeamish about the owl's requirements, it is absolutely vital that he gets the roughage. A disaster once occured to a brood of three barn owls which were taken into custody by a well-meaning farmer's wife who wanted to care for them herself. She was told about their dietary needs but protested that she could not bring herself to calve up mice or day-old chicks for them. She persisted solely with minced beef and tripe; as a result they developed the most profound osteomalacia and only the largest one survived.

If for some reason you can't get hold of chicks or mice, then be sure to wrap the raw beef in soft chicken feathers. But this is a poor substitute for the more natural food. Incidentally, worms, beetles and moths make useful secondary additions to the diet. Your owl should regurgitate a pellet most days.

'Hacking' your orphan back into the wild is rather a long-drawn-out affair. Start taking him into the garden to a suitable post well before he is fully fledged. Play with him, using food items to develop his interest in chasing and catching. It is your job to teach him to hunt. Tie a piece of thread to the tail of a dead mouse. Throw the mouse near the owl and tweak the thread to make the mouse look alive. When the owl takes the mouse let him have it, and of course have scissors ready so that you cut the thread before he swallows it all. (A short knotted bit at the tail won't matter.) Do this every day, lengthening the thread and making it harder for the owl to find the mouse. Drop the bait in longer grass. The object of the exercise is to get the owl used to the idea of finding food in the right kind of mouse habitat.

When your owl has left you and is sleeping out, it is still important to provide him with food every day. You should carry on feeding some three months after the bird has left the nest, taking you probably into September. It is a long time before your owl is completely independent.

Injured Owls

If an owl is sick or groggy on its legs, its chances of recovering health are very slim. However, you may have the chance of treating a bird which has been injured by flying into a wire, or been struck by a vehicle on the road.

If the fracture is at the joint, then we fear that the best advice may be to kill it, because it will inevitably end up with a stiff wing which will keep it grounded for life. But if the fracture is midway between joints there is hope. Dr Leonard Hurrell, who has had a great deal of experience in treating wounded birds of prey, recommends the following technique: fractures of the radius or ulna are treated by immobilisation with plaster of Paris bandage (Gypsona 2in/50mm). There do not appear to be any disadvantages in this method. It can usually be applied with the owl hooded, perhaps under sedation, and held down by an assistant. Two or three thicknesses of the bandage are applied to the flexor aspect along the axis of the bones and further lengths are added to envelop the carpal and elbow joints. While the plaster is still malleable the alignment should be improved as much as possible, and as it sets the wing can be immobilised in the resting position of flexion. The plaster is fairly heavy and may unbalance the casualty for a day or two, but as it has to be kept in a box in any case this does not overcomplicate management.

After-care is tedious but not unduly difficult. Confinement in a dark cardboard box with hand-feeding once or twice a day keeps movement to a minimum. Forced-feeding is often necessary until the plaster is removed. This should be thoroughly soaked with water and will then come off the feathers quite easily. After the first bathe and preen, the plumage looks as good as new.

One of the most difficult things to estimate is the time for a particular fracture to be kept in plaster. A simple fracture of a long bone may take about one week, but a compound fracture will certainly take two to three weeks. If union has not occurred after a month, infection is probably still active, and since the cardboard-box conditions cannot be maintained indefinitely, one has to decide whether there is any future in persisting with treatment.

Appendix 3

OWLS — A SYSTEMATIC LIST

CLASS: AVES
  ORDER: STRIGIFORMES
    FAMILY: *TYTONIDAE*
      SUBFAMILY: *TYTONINAE* (Barn and Grass Owls)
        GENUS: *TYTO*

Tyto alba	Barn Owl
Tyto novaehollandiae	Masked Owl
Tyto sonmagnei	Soumagnes or Madagascar Grass Owl
Tyto tenebricosa	Sooty Owl
Tyto inexspectata	Minahassa Barn Owl
Tyto aurantia	New Britain Barn Owl
Tyto capensis	Common Grass Owl
Tyto rosenbergii	Celebes Barn Owl

      SUBFAMILY: *PHODILINAE* (Bay Owls)
        GENUS: *PHODILUS*

Phodilus badius	Bay Owl
Phodilus prigoginei	Congo Bay Owl

    FAMILY: *STRIGIDAE*
      SUBFAMILY: *BUBONINAE* (Typical Owls)
        GENUS: *OTUS*

Otus asio	Common Screech Owl
Otus choliba	Tropical Screech Owl
Otus watsonii	Tawny-bellied Screech Owl
Otus albogularis	White-throated Screech Owl
Otus atricapillus	Black-capped Screech Owl

Otus guatemalae	Vermiculated Screech Owl
Otus trichopsis	Whiskered or Spotted Screech Owl
Otus cooperi	Pacific Screech Owl
Otus barbarus	Bearded Screech Owl
Otus roboratus	Dark-crowned Screech Owl
Otus nudipes	Puerto Rican Screech Owl
Otus clarkii	Bare-shanked Screech Owl
Otus ingens	Rufescent Screech Owl
Otus flammeolus	Flammulated Owl
Otus scops	Common Scops Owl
Otus bakkamoena	Collared Scops Owl
Otus spilocephalus	Spotted Scops Owl
Otus balli	Andaman Scops Owl
Otus sagittatus	White-fronted Scops Owl
Otus rufescens	Reddish Scops Owl
Otus beccarii	Biak Scops Owl
Otus alfredi	Flores Scops Owl
Otus brookii	Rajah Scops Owl
Otus manadensis	Celebes Scops Owl
Otus silvicola	Lesser Sunda Scops Owl
Otus umbra	Mentaur Scops Owl
Otus icterorhynchus	Cinnamon Scops Owl
Otus gurneyi	Giant Scops Owl
Otus rutilus	Madagascar Scops Owl
Otus leucotis	White-faced Scops Owl
GENUS: *JUBULA*	
Jubula lettii	Maned Owl
GENUS: *LOPHOSTRIX*	
Lophostrix cristata	Crested Owl
GENUS: *BUBO*	
Bubo virginianus	Great Horned Owl
Bubo bubo	Eagle Owl
Bubo africanus	Spotted Eagle Owl
Bubo capensis	Cape Eagle Owl
Bubo lacteus	Milky Eagle Owl
Bubo poensis	Fraser's Eagle Owl
Bubo leucostictus	Akun Eagle Owl

Bubo shelleyi	Shelly's Eagle Owl
Bubo sumatrana	Malay Eagle Owl
Bubo philippensis	Philippine Eagle Owl
Bubo nipalensis	Forest Eagle Owl
Bubo coromandus	Dusky Eagle Owl
GENUS: *KETUPA*	
Ketupa ketupa	Malay Fish Owl
Ketupa zeylonensis	Brown Fish Owl
Ketupa flavipes	Tawny Fish Owl
Ketupa blakistoni	Blakiston's Fish Owl
GENUS: *SCOTOPELIA*	
Scotopelia bouvieri	Vermiculated Fishing Owl
Scotopelia peli	Pel's Fishing Owl
Scotopelia ussheri	Rufous Fishing Owl
GENUS: *PULSATRIX*	
Pulsatrix perspicillata	Spectacled Owl
Pulsatrix melanota	Rusty-barred Owl
Pulsatrix koeniswaldiana	White-chinned Owl
GENUS: *NYCTEA*	
Nyctea scandiaca	Snowy Owl
GENUS: *SURNIA*	
Surnia ulula	Hawk Owl
GENUS: *GLAUCIDIUM*	
Glaucidium brasilianum	Ferruginous Pigmy Owl
Glaucidium gnoma	Northern Pigmy Owl
Glaucidium minutissimum	Least Pigmy Owl
Glaucidium jardinii	Andean Pigmy Owl
Glaucidium passerinum	Cuban Pigmy Owl
Glaucidium siju	Eurasian Pigmy Owl
Glaucidium tephronotum	Red-chested Owlet
Glaucidium sjöstedti	Chestnut-backed Owlet
Glaucidium radiatum	Jungle Owlet
Glaucidium perlatum	Pearl-spotted Owlet
Glaucidium capense	Barred Owlet
Glaucidium brodiei	Collared Owlet
Glaucidium cuculoides	Cuckoo Owlet
GENUS: *MICRATHENE*	
Micrathene whitneyi	Elf Owl

GENUS: *UROGLAUX*

Uroglaux dimorpha	New Guinea Hawk Owl

GENUS: *NINOX*

Ninox connivens	Barking Owl
Ninox novaeseelandiae	Boobook or Spotted Hawk Owl
Ninox strenua	Great Hawk Owl
Ninox rufa	Rufous Hawk Owl
Ninox odiosa	New Britain Hawk Owl
Ninox meeki	Admiralty Islands Hawk Owl
Ninox punctulata	Speckled Hawk Owl
Ninox squampilia	Moluccan Hawk Owl
Ninox theomacha	Sooty-backed Hawk Owl
Ninox jacquinota	Solomon Islands Hawk Owl
Ninox solomonis	New Ireland Hawk Owl
Ninox perversa	Ochre-bellied Hawk Owl
Ninox scutulata	Oriental Hawk Owl
Ninox affinis	Andaman Hawk Owl
Ninox philippensis	Philippine Hawk Owl
Ninox superciliaris	Madagascar Hawk Owl

GENUS: *GYMNOGLAUX*

Gymnoglaux lawrencii	Bare-legged Owl

GENUS: *SCELOGLAUX*

Sceloglaux albifacies	Laughing Owl

GENUS: *ATHENE*

Athene noctua	Little Owl
Athene brama	Spotted Owlet
Athene blewitti	Forest Spotted Owlet

GENUS: *SPEOTYTO*

Speotyto cunicularia	Burrowing Owl

GENUS: *CICCÀBA*

Ciccaba virgata	Mottled Owl
Ciccaba nigrolineata	Black-and-white Owl
Ciccaba huhula	Black-banded Owl
Ciccaba albitarsus	Rufous-banded Owl
Ciccaba woodfordii	African Wood Owl

SUBFAMILY: *STRIGINAE*

GENUS: *STRIX*

Strix varia	Barred Owl

Strix hylophila	Brazilian Owl
Strix rufipes	Rufous-legged Owl
Strix occidentalis	Spotted Owl
Strix nebulosa	Great Gray or Lapland Owl
Strix aluco	Tawny Owl
Strix uralensis	Ural Owl
Strix butleri	Hume's Tawny Owl
Strix leptogrammica	Brown Wood Owl
Strix ocellata	Mottled Wood Owl
Strix seloputo	Spotted Wood Owl
GENUS: *RHINOPTYNX*	
Rhinoptynx clamator	Striped Owl
GENUS: *ASIO*	
Asio otus	Long-eared Owl
Asio stygius	Stygian Owl
Asio abyssinicus	Abyssinian Long-eared Owl
Asio madagascariensis	Madagascar Long-eared Owl
Asio flammeus	Short-eared Owl
Asio capensis	African Marsh Owl
GENUS: *PSEUDOSCOPS*	
Pseudoscops grammicus	Jamaican Owl
GENUS: *NESASIO*	
Nesasio solomonensis	Fearful Owl
GENUS: *AEGOLIUS*	
Aegolius acadius	Saw-whet Owl
Aegolius ridgwayi	Unspotted Saw-whet Owl
Aegolius harrisii	Buff-fronted Owl
Aegolius funereus	Boreal or Tengmalm's Owl

Reference Sources

Armstrong, E.A. *A Study of Bird Song* (Oxford, 1963)
  The Folklore of Birds (1968)
Arvill, R. *Man and Environment* (1967)
Austin, O.L. and Singer, A. *Birds of the World* (1961)
Bannerman, D.A. *The Birds of the British Isles*, Vol 4 (Edinburgh, 1955)
Berg, W., Johnels, A., Sjöstrand, B. and Westermark, T. 'Mercury contents in feathers of Swedish birds from the past 100 years', *Oikos*, 17 (1966), 71–83
Beven, G. 'The Food of Tawny Owls in London'. London Bird Report 29, (1964), 56–72
Bonner, Campbell. *Studies in Magical Amulets* (Michigan, 1950)
Brusewitz, G. *Hunting* (1969)
Buller, Sir W.L. *Birds of New Zealand*, ed E.G. Turbot (1967)
Bunn, D.S., Warburton, A.B. and Wilson, R.D.S. *The Barn Owl* (T & A.D. Poyser 1982)
Cloudsley-Thompson, J.L. *The Zoology of Tropical Africa* (1969)
Collav, N.J. and Andrew P. *Birds to watch* (ICBP Technical Pubs No 8 1988)
Craighead, J.J. and F.C. *Hawks, Owls and Wildlife* (Harrisburg, Pa, 1956)
Cramp, S. 'Toxic chemicals and birds of prey', *British Birds*, 56 no 4 (1963), 124–39
Cramp, S. and Tomlins, A.D. 'The birds of inner London 1951–65', *British Birds*, 59 no 6 (1966), 209–33
Curry-Lindahl, K. 'Berguvens, *Bubo bubo* (1), förehomst i Sverige jainte något om dess biologi', *Vår Fågelrärld*, 9 (1950), 113–65

'The reintroduction of eagle owls in Sweden', *Annual Report 1964 of the Ornamental Pheasant Trust and Norfolk Wildlife Park* (1964), 31–3

Curtis, W.E. 'Quantitative Studies of Vision of Owls', (PhD thesis, Cornell University, 1952)

Darwin, Charles. *More Letters*, Vol 1 (1905)

Elton, C.S. *The Pattern of Animal Communities* (1966)

Falla, R.A., Sibson, R.B. and Turbott, E.G. *A field guide to the birds of New Zealand and outlying islands* (1966)

Fisher, J., Simon, N. and Vincent, J. *The Red Book* (1969)

Fitter, R.S.R. *London's Natural History* (1945)

Fuller, E. *Extinct Birds* (Viking/Rainbird 1987)

Fuller, T. *Gnomologia* (1732)

Gibson, F. *Superstitions about Animals* (New York, 1904)

de Givry, G. *Witchcraft, Magic and Alchemy* (1931)

Glegg, W.E. *A History of the Birds of Essex* (1929)

Glue, D.E. 'Prey taken by the Barn Owl in England and Wales', *Bird Study*, 14 no 3 (1967), 169–83

Greenway, J.C. *Extinct and Vanishing Birds of the World* (New York, 1967)

Gross, A.O. 'Cyclic invasions of the snowy owl and the migration of 1945–1946', *Auk*, 64 (1947), 584–601

Grossman, M.L. and Hamlet, J. *Birds of Prey of the World* (1965)

de Gobernatis, Angelo. *Zoological Mythology* (1872)

Gurney, J.H. *Early annals of Ornithology* (1921)

Hagen, Y. 'Eruption of hawk owls in Fennoscandia 1950–51', *Sterna*, 24 (1956), 1–22

'Snougla på Hardangervidda sommeren 1959' (The snowy owl on Hardangervidda in the summer of 1959), *Meddeleser fra statens Viltundersøkelser*, Series 2 no 7 (1960), English summary

Hammerstrom, F. 'The use of Great Horned owls in catching marsh hawks', *Proc XIII Int Orn Congr* (1963), 866–9

Harting, J.E. *The Ornithology of Shakespeare* (1871)

Hibbert-Ware, A. 'Report of the Little Owl Food Enquiry 1936–37', *British Birds*, 31 (1937), 162–87, 205–29, 249–64

Höglund, N.H. 'Über die Ernährung des Uhus *Bubo bubo* Lin in Scheseden wahrend der Brutzeit', *Viltrevy-Swedish Wildlife*, 4 no 2 (1966)

Honer, M.R. 'Observations on the Barn owl (*Tyto alba guttata*) in the Netherlands in relation to its ecology and population fluctuations', *Ardea*, 51 (1963), 158–95

Hosking, E.J. and Newberry, C.W. *Birds of the Night* (1945)

Hultkrantz, Åke. *Concepts of soul among North American Indians* (Sweden, 1953)

Hurrell, L.H. *Wild Raptor Casualties* (Slapton, Devon, 1968)

ICBP *Report on the Working Conference on Birds of Prey and Owls* (Caen, France, 1964)

Jefferies, D.J. and Prestt, I. 'Post-mortems of peregrines and lanners with particular reference to organochlorine residues', *British Birds*, 59 no 2 (1966), 49–64

Lack, D. *Population Studies of Birds* (Oxford, 1966)

Landsborough Thomson, Sir A. *A New Dictionary of Birds* (1964)

Lang, Andrew. *Custom and Myth* (1901)

Lindblat, J. *I Ugglemarker* (Stockholm, 1967)

Lockie, J.D. 'The breeding habits of short-eared owls after a vole plague', *Bird Study*, 2 (1955), 53–69

Lucas, J. *International Zoo Yearbook*, Vol 10 (1970)

Marples, B.J. 'A study of the little owl (*Athene noctua*) in New Zealand', *Trans Proc Roy Soc NZ*, 72 (1942), 237–52

Mellanby, K. *Pesticides and Pollution* (1967)

Mikkola, H. *Owls of Europe* (T & A.D. Poyser 1983)

Montier, D. 'A survey of the Breeding Distribution of the kestrel, barn owl and tawny owl in the London area in 1967', *The London Bird Report*, 32 (1968), 81–92

Moore, N.W. *Ecology and the Industrial Society*, 5th Symp Brit Ecolog Soc (1965)

Morris, P. 'Owl Pellets', *Animals*, 12 no 5 (1969), 208–10
The Nature Conservancy Progress 1964–68 (1968)

O'Connor, R. and Shrubb, M. *Farming and Birds* (CUP 1986)

Parslow, J.L.F. 'Changes in status among breeding birds in Britain in Ireland', part 3, *British Birds*, 60 no 5 (1967), 177–202

Payne, R.S. 'How the barn owl locates prey by hearing', *The Living Bird*, 1 (1962), 151–89

Peters, J.L. *Check-List of birds of the world*, Vol 4 (Harvard, 1940)

Philipson, W.R. and Doncaster, C.C. 'Birds seen in the North Atlantic', *British Birds*, 44 no 1 (1951), 11–13

Phipson, Emma. *Animal Lore of Shakespeare's Time* (1883)

Prestt, I. 'An enquiry into the recent breeding status of some of the smaller birds of prey and crows in Britain', *Bird Study*, 12 no 3, 196–221

Prestt, I. and Bell, A.A. 'An objective method in recording breeding distribution of common birds of prey in Britain', *Bird Study*, 13 no 4, 227–83

Randle, W. and Austing, R. 'Ecological notes on long-eared and saw-whet owls in south-western Ohio', *Ecology*, 33 (1952), 422–6

Ratcliffe, D.A. 'Decrease in eggshell weight in certain birds of prey', *Nature*, 215 no 5097 (1967), 208

Ray, John. *Compleat Collection of English Proverbs* (1670)

Robinson, M. and Dustin Becker, C. 'Snowy Owls in Fetlar' *British Birds* 79 (1986), 228–242

Robinson, P. *The Poets' Birds* (1883)

RSPB. *The fifth report of the Joint Committee of the British Trust for Ornithology and the Royal Society for the Protection of Birds on Toxic Chemicals*, August 1963–July 1964 (1965)

Russell, W.M.S. *Man, Nature and History* (1967)

Schwartzkopff, J. 'Morphological and Physiological properties of the auditory system in birds', *Proc XIII Intern Ornith Congr* (1963), 1059–68

Shawyer, C.R. *The Barn Owl in the British Isles* (The Hawk Trust 1987)

Sparks, J.H. *Bird Behaviour* (1969)

Southern, H.N. 'Tawny owls and their prey', *Ibis*, 96 (1954), 384–410

Southern, H.N., Vaughan, R. and Muir, R.C. 'The behaviour of young tawny owls after fledging', *Bird Study*, 1, 101–10

Voous, K.H. *Atlas of European Birds* (1960)

   'Wood owls of the genera *Strix* and *Ciccaba*', *Zoölogische Mededelingen*, 39 (1964), 471

Watkins, M.G. *Gleanings from the Natural History of the Ancients* (1885)

Watson, A. 'The behaviour, breeding and food ecology of the snowy owl, *Nyctea scandiaca*', *Ibis*, 99 (1957), 418–62

Wetmore, A. 'Remains of birds from caves in the Republic of Haiti', *Smithsonian Misc Collections*, 74 no 4 (1922)

Welty, J.C. *The Life of Birds* (1964)

Willock, T. 'The water-dripping owl', *Animals*, 12 no 4 (1969), 184

Acknowledgements

We have been helped a great deal in gathering material for this book. The late James Fisher advised on some points concerning fossil owls. Professor J.B. Fry, of the Phonetics Department, University College, London, kindly arranged to have spectrograms made of the hoots of a number of owl species. Hilary Soper was indefatigable in her search for owl legends and 'owliana'. Amongst others, John Parslow, then of the Nature Conservancy Council, and Mike Kendall of the BBC's Natural History Unit read a first draft and made many helpful suggestions, although they are not responsible for the shortcomings of the final version.

John Sparks
Tony Soper

Index

References to illustrations are shown *in italic*: photographs shown in **bold**.